American Racism

Black Power in a White World

By: CK Justice

First Printing: 2019
Cover Design: PukaPrat Ink

ISBN for Paperback: 9781793257000

For more real talk about current events and other issues affecting America,
please check out my blog and join my email list at
www.Angrypatriot42.com

You can also follow me on twitter
@CKJustice_AP42

Or on Facebook
Facebook.com/CKJusticeAP42

<u>Dedication</u>

This book is dedicated to my second child, E.O. She makes me laugh and enjoy life. She is the reason I fight for a better tomorrow.   I will always love you. Be good. Stay safe. Always be ready to fight against evil.

Table of Contents

<u>Foreword</u>

Black Power.
Black Pride.
Brotherhood.

But is that enough in a racist world? Or should we seek to change it? There is a deep history of racism in this country. Where did it come from? Why do people ignore it? Why are the people in power not helping? This book answers those questions. The history of racism in America is traced from its beginnings, through the sordid past, and into the present turmoil. Racism is rampant in America, but what will the future hold?

There is hope. There is **power** in our history, **power** in knowledge, and the **power** within us of self-determination and will. We have the ability to change ourselves, to change our segment of society, and ultimately to change America.

The key to ending the vicious cycle of racism is found here…

Chapter 1: What is Racism Anyway?

The term racist has been flung about so often in our society that it seems to have lost its meaning. People today seem to have many ideas about what it means ranging from "I don't like what you said" all the way to the worst possible insult of "you're a Nazi". Words mean something and words can be very powerful when used correctly. Oftentimes the difference between sounding like an idiot and being a great orator is not merely the passion of the speaker but the way the words are used.

A person might foam at the mouth and scream till their face turns red that "everyone who voted for [insert policy or person here] is a racist!!" That person may appear deranged, a few fries short of a happy meal, or merely stupid for making a blanket statement like that.

However, someone may make the claim that the entire society, not just a certain group of people, is racist by putting words together in such a way as to inspire people to change. It might sound something like this,

"I say to you today, my friends, so even though we face the difficulties of today and tomorrow, I still have a dream. It is a dream deeply rooted in the American dream. I have a dream that one day this nation will rise up and live out the true meaning of its creed: 'We hold these truths to be self-evident: that all men are created equal.'" – Dr. Martin Luther King Jr.

Dr. Martin Luther King Jr. understood that the society he lived in was racist and that it often led to violence. This is precisely why he chose the words he did. He chose to combat violence with peace and used words that inspired people to positive change not destructive change. His intelligence was demonstrated not only in the way he presented himself but also in the words he chose to use.

Dr. King made sure to present himself as a respectful and a respectable person by being clean and courteous in his appearance and attitude. The words he used demonstrated his understanding of what they meant and he put them together in a way that was almost poetic as well. Rather than appearing as a red faced, spitting, angry person, he came across as a passionate intelligent leader.

Racism is not merely a word to use against a person, it is an idea that begins in one's mind and eventually permeates the person's attitude and actions throughout their life. The layman's definition of racism is simply judging someone based on the color of their skin and not on whom they really are or what they do or say.

Here are a few official definitions of the word:

Dictionary.com - "Racism is a belief or doctrine that inherent differences among the various human racial groups determine cultural or individual achievement, usually involving the idea that one's own race is superior and has the right to dominate others or that a particular racial group is inferior to the others."

Merriam-webster.com - "A belief that race is the primary determinant of human traits and capacities and that racial differences produce an inherent superiority of a particular race, racial prejudice or discrimination"

Google - "The belief that all members of each race possess characteristics or abilities specific to that race, especially so as to distinguish it as inferior or superior to another race or races"

Racism is intellectually and scientifically laughable. The sad thing is that it is so pervasive that it is a real issue that needs to be addressed. Any reasonable person should look at the idea of racism as completely ridiculous and without merit. Seriously take a look at the common definitions of racism and try to explain to someone that their ability to be a good or bad person is determined by the color of their skin.

How astonishing would it be if we were to determine someone's ability to get a job by something so superficial as the length of their nose, the color of their eyes, how tall they are, or what color shoes they wear. Yet many cultures, and many times in history, mankind has chosen to determine things like citizenship, voting rights, ability to get a job, or even the right to life, merely based on the color of one's skin.

Intellectually, this idea of skin color determining behavior or a person's worth is a completely ridiculous argument without any merit. Someone might be able to anecdotally cite experiences they have had with people who happen to be all the same color, but that is a stereotype based on limited data. Anyone who honestly believes that the color of something or someone makes it inherently less worthy is simply intellectually dishonest and completely illogical.

The same thoughts apply to the idea of science as it pertains to racism. The character of someone as well as their upbringing makes them choose to do right or wrong things. A person's abilities and accomplishments are likewise learned and earned, not based on merely genetics. Skin color scientifically plays no role in anything other than possibly melatonin or skin diseases. The only role skin color plays in reality is whether someone finds it aesthetically pleasing or not.

<u>Discrimination and Stereotypes</u>

The cry of racism needs to be used sparingly for only real cases of racism or else it dilutes the charge. If everyone is charged with racism anytime they disagree with someone of a different skin color, then everyone is racist and who really cares? It is an evil charge and ought to only be used when people are truly deserving of it.

There are several concepts that people need to understand when it comes to leveling this charge of racism. The idea of discrimination and also that of a valid stereotype needs to be understood properly lest we charge someone with racism unfairly. Many acts may appear as racism to those who look at color first, however; color should not be the first thing that determines a situation or action. Many stereotypes and acts of discrimination are actually valid.

Let's take a look at the definition of discrimination first.

Discrimination:

Merriam-Webster.com- 1. The act, practice, or an instance of discriminating categorically rather than individually. 2. The quality or power of finely distinguishing.

Google.com - Recognition and understanding of the difference between one thing and another.

Dictionary.com – 1. An act or instance of making a distinction. 2. Treatment or consideration of, or making a distinction in favor of or against, a person or thing based on the group, class, or category to which that person or thing belongs rather than on individual merit: racial and religious intolerance and discrimination. 3. The power of making fine distinctions; discriminating judgment: She chose the colors with great discrimination.

Everybody discriminates. It is usually a good thing even though people often think of it as evil. Most people discriminate with the foods they eat. Wine connoisseurs are known for their "discriminating taste". I discriminate on what toppings to put on my pizza as I hate anchovies, peppers, and pineapple. We all discriminate on who we are willing to go out on a date with. Some people prefer to only date people of a certain height. Women typically don't like to date guys shorter than them. Guys sometimes only date girls with certain hair colors. People discriminate based on all sorts of body types and yes, even skin color. There is nothing wrong with that and it is most often NOT racist in nature.

People are individually attracted to different things for a variety of reasons and there is nothing wrong with that. Some people are only attracted to people of their race, some people are only attracted to those of a different skin color and they choose not to date their own race. This is a healthy form of discrimination because it requires a person to know themselves and their own desires. As long as it is not based on racism, discrimination is normal and in some instances the preferred way to live.

Sometimes, we even discriminate based on religion because we choose to only go to a certain type of church. Discrimination is also used when hiring people. Businesses have a hiring process and get to choose (yes, they actually DO discriminate) who they will and who they will not hire. I would even advocate that any business should be allowed to discriminate on ANY basis (religious, skin color, gender, etc.) because the free market will decide if their goods or services are of important enough value to ignore that discrimination. After all, if you need food, and they can provide it at a reasonable price, then your stomach doesn't care if they like your skin color or not.

The reverse side of that coin is that a business exists to make money. In order to make money, they must cater to as many people as possible. If a business excludes a certain demographic, on a discriminatory basis, they are looking for a certain niche of consumers. For instance, if Big and Tall advertised to short petite people, that would not make sense. Their niche is people that are big and tall, not short and petite. It would not make sense for them to spend money trying to get people into their stores who will not be able to find anything to buy. That store actually discriminates against short and petite people and there is nothing wrong with that. They are not saying that those people are lesser human beings; they have merely chosen to seek out a certain type of consumer.

If however, a business is discriminating because they are racist then that is clearly wrong. They not only are excluding that entire race from being potential customers, but they are also going to lose customers of every other race. Decent human beings of all colors would boycott that business until they could no longer afford to maintain a store. That would be discriminating in a good way, to help prevent the bad discrimination based on race.

The discrimination against that store is clearly not racism, but an act to support equality of races. That is capitalism at its finest! In America, you can choose a different company and make the racist one go out of business because they are mean! Yay America, you can actually financially punish someone for bad behavior, why pay the government to do it for you?

The government regulations, laws, restrictions on business, and the manpower required to enforce those laws and monitor businesses should be minimized. Let the free market decide what a business can or cannot do. The idea that government can dictate morals to people is the road towards tyranny. A free society should always lean towards correcting social issues socially, not through laws if it can be avoided. We should be discriminating enough to spend our money in a way that incentivizes businesses to do the right thing.

Discrimination is usually done for a specific purpose. Whether it is dating, the foods you eat, where you shop, what friends you choose to have, or what religion you choose, a discriminating person is not necessarily racist. If someone chooses to only have honest and hardworking people as friends and they happen to all be Latino, is that racist? No, the skin color has nothing to do with it. If someone chooses to only have Latino friends because they think all white people are dishonest, is that racist? Yes. By the definition of the word racist, they are making a judgment merely based on the color of someone's skin.

The point is simply this; don't allow yourself to call someone a racist merely because the person they are discriminating against has a different skin color. There are many good reasons to discriminate, and skin color might actually have had nothing to do with it.

Another good reason for discrimination could be merely personal preference not born out of racism. For instance, if my favorite waitress at the restaurant I go to everyday happens to be white despite the majority of waitresses being black, it would be foolish for you to call me racist based on skin color alone.

The more obvious reason might be that she wears low cut shirts and always flirts with me! Nobody knows what somebody is thinking or why someone chooses to discriminate unless they tell you or there is some other evidence. Do not be so quick to judge another person.

<u>Stereotype</u>

The other word that we need to understand before we go calling people racist is the word stereotype. A stereotype is based on data and observation of actual events and persons.

Here are some common definitions of Stereotype:

Google-"A widely held but fixed and oversimplified image or idea of a particular type of person or thing."

Merriam-Webster.com-"To believe unfairly that all people or things with a particular characteristic are the same"

Dictionary.com-"A simplified and standardized conception or image invested with special meaning and held in common by members of a group"

For example, I am from Indiana and I have also lived in Georgia, Virginia, New Mexico, Missouri, and Arizona. Over the course of 20 some years of driving in these states, I have reached the limited data conclusion that Indiana drivers are the most polite drivers. They will let you switch lanes or get in front of them on the road, and they also typically wave a thank you when you let them in front of you. That is a stereotype that is based on things and people that I have actually seen. It doesn't hold true 100% of the time, but it is GENERALLY true from my experience.

It is a valid stereotype based off of my experiences but it is not racist. Nobody can say that my comment proves I hate Mexicans. Just because Indiana is comprised of mostly white people does not mean that is why I think Indiana drivers are the best. That is an illogical and frankly stupid conclusion based on poor reasoning.

Also, that stereotype is based off a limited subset of only six out of fifty states. This is what makes it a stereotype because it cannot be applied to the whole population. My stereotype about drivers in Indiana is a "simplified" conception of a common group of people. It is also unfair because not all drivers in Indiana are good, nor are all drivers in others states necessarily worse. However, this is a valid stereotype based on the people and situations that I have encountered.

I know a girl who has worked in retail her whole life and while working in one particular city as a manager, she noticed that the majority of Hispanic people that entered her store usually ended up stealing things. She formed a stereotype based on actual events that happened in her life, that Hispanics were thieves and that she shouldn't trust them. Her belief is not racist. Her stereotype can be changed if she meets more Hispanics that DON'T steal because she does not hold a core belief that she is better than them. She is not racist; she has formed a factual stereotype because in her line of work, in that populace, it was GENERALLY TRUE. Remember that stereotypes are based on common traits found in a group, population, class, gender, etc. and not merely race.

An example of a good racial stereotype is that Asians are good at math. This comes about because in general the Asian culture places more emphasis on schooling and knowledge than many other cultures. This means, that in general, if you meet an Asian they will probably be more scholarly (and thus better at math) than the average American.

A stereotype of black culture is that African-Americans have the highest rate of single-parent homes of any race in America. Kidscount.org puts the number at 65% of black families. This is not a racist statistic. This is a fact. Facts are not racist. This is a statistic which backs up the stereotype. When speaking about black families in America this is a completely valid fact to bring up, but it is merely a generic stereotype. If you see a black man and immediately judge him as someone who is a bad father who does not take care of his kids, then you are making a racist judgment based on the color of his skin.

To sum up stereotypes, they are simply a generalization of either a good or bad trait about a group of people. A stereotype is something generally believed about a group but something that can be demonstrated to be false on an individual basis. Someone who believes a stereotype or makes a statement about the nature of a certain group of people may or may not be racist.

A logical adult will look deeper into the facts and statistics and understand that a stereotypical statement is based on limited data and is not always true. A racist statement is different in two ways. One, a racist statement makes a claim based ONLY on skin color and then tries to use random data or anecdotal evidence to back it up. Two, a racist statement makes a claim that it is always true BECAUSE of skin color, with maybe a few exceptions.

For example: the statement that "white men cause the majority of spouse abuse in America" could be a racist statement or it could be a stereotype based on facts. It would require that the hearer take this statement in context and understand the intent of the person making the statement to understand which of those two things it is.

If the person making the statement happens to be making the case, that white men are naturally abusive people, then the context of the statement is that of race determining character. That is the very definition of racism. That person has made a judgment on an entire race of people merely based on the color of their skin. That is a horrible, untrue, and unjust statement to make and it actually shows the evil nature of the person making the statement.

However, if the context is that the person is making a generalization that white men are statistically more prone to lashing out angrily at their spouse than other races in America, then that is a stereotype and the data would need to be examined. In fact, the Bureau of Justice keeps track of these statistics and one would have to look at overall numbers find out if this claim was true.

The statistical data in a white majority country should show that the majority of crimes are committed by whites. However, if you break it down by percentages, you find a much more accurate number. According to Census.gov in 2000 whites made up 81.1% of the U.S.A. population and blacks made up 12.7% of the population. If spousal abuse by whites was higher by percentage of population (for example 85% white and only 7% black) then this stereotype would be true. In fact, the Bureau of Justice Statistics shows that spouse abuse offenders in the time period from 1998 to 2002 were 82.5% white and 11.5% black. Statistically, for that time period in America, the stereotype that whites committed more spouse abuse crimes by percentage of population than blacks is in fact true by approximately one percentage point.[1] The original statement is actually a factual stereotype.

Let us get back to the main point. We should not be so quick to call people racist. Please look at facts and argue points of logical discussion instead of name calling. If you feel it necessary to name call, please be factual. Remember that everyone discriminates, and that is a normal human thing to do. Most people have stereotypes and those are based on facts and actual experiences. Few people actually believe that they are superior simply because of their race. If they do, they are guilty of racism and deserving of that evil label. Be smart. Don't be ignorant, and be careful of throwing around labels merely because you disagree with someone.

<u>Core Beliefs</u>

The point of racism is not to be intentionally mean or destructive, but racism in

28

practicality almost always leads to those ends. A racist person holds a core value or belief about human beings in general that can't help but play itself out in words and actions. It is similar to a deeply held religious conviction in that it becomes part of a person's character.

When someone holds a core belief, it means that it is a primary cause for other beliefs and that it drives their thoughts and actions. This is known as a World View and it is how the person begins to see everything in their life. It is similar to wearing sun glasses with a particular hue to them. Everything takes on that color/hue and you begin to see the world only from that perspective. In this case, everything in life starts to only make sense based on the color of people's skin.

For instance, if one of my core beliefs was that math was a social construct of an authoritarian patriarchy, then it would drive many of my actions in life. I would probably not handle money well, and would end up with an overdrawn checking account and not be able to pay bills. I may not show up on time for things and eventually lose my job. My core belief that math wasn't something I needed to learn or follow would filter through into my everyday actions in many ways.

Exercising at a gym would be almost impossible because trying to balance out weights on each side of a bar would be difficult without math. I might use only three pound weights and tell the world that I could bench three hundred pounds because I refuse to believe that the number three actually stands for three. Cooking would be all but impossible without the proper ratio of ingredients. Driving a certain speed down the road would be dangerous with someone who doesn't believe in math because their idea of a speed limit would be arbitrary from one day to the next. Someone who doesn't believe in math like this would quickly find out that their belief affects all areas of their life.

When a belief is a core value, one cannot help but act on that belief in every facet of life. The point is simply this; a core belief permeates your whole life. One's core beliefs help them make decisions in every area, from personal relationships, to business, to pleasure.

Racism has as its core belief, one of two ideas. A racist person either believes that one particular skin color is inferior to another, or that one particular skin color is superior to another. The majority of the time, the superiority complex is built around the skin color of the racist person. The inferiority belief is usually built around the skin color of someone that is despised by the racist person. Most of the time, these two beliefs go hand in hand. Rarely, but becoming more common in Western cultures, do people have the inferiority complex about their own race.

The belief that one is superior to another comes from one of the baser instincts of mankind. It feeds into the selfishness of man by allowing him to think that vast groups of people don't deserve what he/she has. This makes the person feel that they have an inerrant and indisputable right to feel superior to other races merely because they were born a certain color. They feel special and then must continually feed that world view with data to maintain that feeling. Every time someone of their particular skin color accomplishes something special, they attribute it to their "superiority". Every time someone of another race is caught doing something particularly stupid or evil, that is attributed to their skin color as well. This serves to prove to the racist person that they are correct, their race is superior. Anything that does not fit the narrative is merely discarded or ignored as an anomaly.

Hitler viewed his "Master Race" as superior to all others and thus the inferior races had to be eliminated. The KKK believes the white race is superior and Jews and blacks are inferior. Islam views the Jewish race as particularly inferior to all others. Racism comes in many stripes, but the core beliefs of inferiority and superiority are present every time. It doesn't matter which race or group of people it is, or which group they are racist against, they all have the same core beliefs.

The inferiority complex tied to one's self is usually the result of intense indoctrination. This is similar to Stockholm Syndrome where someone captivated and abused begins to fall in love with their captor. That type of racism is particularly evil in that it twists the very nature of humans, which is to love themselves. The amount of lies and twisted logic it takes to make someone loathe themselves or their race of people simply based on skin color is extraordinary. That someone would willingly subject themselves to this type of indoctrination in a free society is puzzling.

When someone has a core belief it has to affect their actions or they eventually stop believing it and form a new core belief. This is why racism is so dangerous. It generally leads to unjust actions against individuals or entire groups of people simply based on the color of their skin. In America, everyone has the right to believe what they want. It is actions that affect others, and actions that society can make laws against, to try to keep society civil.

A racist may say that they do not want to hurt others, but their core beliefs will eventually force them to do something based on those beliefs. A racist may become a banker and eventually, if given the opportunity, they may make a lending decision based on that belief. They may choose to not make a home loan to, say, a Hispanic person who is qualified and deserving of it, simply because they don't like Hispanics. This is the point that their beliefs have crossed the line and hurt someone. Thankfully, in America, this is illegal and we have a justice system that already addresses it.

A person's core beliefs about human beings will affect who they choose as friends, who they date, where they live, who they are willing to work with, who they marry, and every social interaction in life. Racism as a core belief is flawed in every way and ought to be repudiated every time it rears its ugly head. It does not matter what color it is used against, racism is evil in that it allows injustices simply based on color without regard to facts about a person.

A free society dares not enact laws against a person's thoughts or beliefs lest it become free no longer. However, a free society can shun those evil beliefs and prosecute injustices with appropriate laws. This in turn will serve as a deterrent to future acts of racism. The only other thing that can be done to prevent evil thoughts is to properly educate society as to the evils of racism with actual facts and evidence from history so that it is not repeated. Slavery, the Holocaust, genocides, and many other things in human history ought to be taught in every school. Education is the key. We cannot and must not attempt to legislate against ignorance, but we should fight it and refute it every time we see it.

Anyone that believes skin color is more important than character and actions is foolish. As Dr. Martin Luther King, Jr. said,

"I have a dream that my four little children will one day live in a nation where they will not be judged by the color of their skin, but by the content of their character."

Chapter 2: Racism in America's Past

America is a great nation and one that we should be happy to live in. If you don't think it is, there are two things you should consider. The first thing is that America is the one nation that everyone in the world is trying to get into. One needs only to look at all the legal immigrants (nearly 1,000,000 per year) and the many nations they come from to see that literally every race of people is currently trying to get into this country. That is not to mention all the illegal ones that pour into this country from Canada, Syria, Mexico, Central and South America, and other countries. The United States of America is so large and has such a porous border that people from all over the world book flights to Canada and Mexico just to sneak into this country. Ask yourself, if America is so bad, why does everyone want to come here?

The second thing you should consider if you do not think America is the best country to live in is that it is still a free country. There are no walls with guards or guard towers keeping you here. You can walk, fly, drive, or sail out of this country without fear of being forced to stay. Go visit another country that you think is better for a year or two and then make your decision. If you still feel that America is not the best country to live in, then revoke your citizenship and stay out. Why be unhappy?

That being said; America, like any other nation, has a past built on conquering the land, developing the country and citizenry, and forming its laws and society. During the development of this society, there have been times in America's history that are shameful. We would do well to remember it, teach the history, and learn from the past.

Several famous people have stated this different ways but George Santayana puts it this way,

"Those who cannot remember the past are condemned to repeat it." [2]

That goes for humanity as a whole and America as a nation. Those who would destroy the past or write it out of history books are creating a problem and not actually correcting history. This chapter takes a look at some of America's history that is unsavory and attempts to see if America has learned from it.

There is a uniqueness to America's history of discrimination and even racism that is a combination of those things with a bit of something else. It has actually been used as a tool by politicians. By that, I mean that politicians have encouraged racism and made laws to enable racism to advance their own goals. In America, racism has been pushed the majority of the time, by those in power. The media, government, and in modern times the education centers have all used racism as a means to an end. There will be more on that later.

Let's take a look at America's history.

<u>American Indians</u>

This country was founded first by accidental discovery by explorers such as Leif Erikson some five hundred years or so before the famous "discovery" of Christopher Columbus. Erikson left a small outpost/village in what he called Vinland, but was unable to maintain it due to skirmishes with the native populations (what we call Indians). Later, Europeans "discovered" this new continent, the most remembered explorer being Columbus in 1492. As has happened since the dawn of time, a discovery of new land led to the attempted settlement by the discoverers.

This led to clashes with various tribes of Natives. It wasn't until widespread exploration of this New World and subsequent towns and outposts that the native population realized that they were in fact being invaded and they needed to organize and fight back. This led to a full on war, the likes of which have been fought for eons between land dwellers and those who would seek to take over that land.

The Wild West was full of atrocities committed by different tribes of Native Americans and it came to be common for European Settlers to expect any Native to attempt to kill them upon first contact. Some tribes were peaceful, but by and large, the Indian population came from a different culture built on mistrust and warfare. Even treaties were seen differently and not understood by the invaders.

The Spaniards, British, and French all set the standard of mistrust and misuse of the Native populations and in turn, those tribes retaliated. There were no innocent sides in this cultural war. Sure, anyone can provide anecdotes here or there of some innocent that was slaughtered by the white man or by the red man, but by and large both sides murdered people and both sides had reason to retaliate when that happened.

There are plenty of stories of innocent wagon trains wiped out by Indians, homesteads burned, women raped and scalped, children taken away into captivity, and thousands of innocent whites attacked and killed by different Native American tribes. The stories of the Blackfoot and Apache Indians use of excruciating torture are legendary and would put ISIS to shame for their lack of inventiveness.

By the same token, there are stories of the white men's abuse and murder as well. The rape of Indian women was not seen as quite as bad as the rape of white women because they were just "savages". The retaliation and murder of women and children was sometimes seen as justified because of what the Indians had done. Later, after America was formed, there were treaties that were not honored and eventually the overwhelming tide of explorers and new Europeans pushed the Indians off their lands.

The final clashes of the dying American Indian way of life came too late to accomplish much. The remaining tribes tried to unite after they were weakened beyond repair and the new American civilization utterly destroyed them. The remaining Indians were forced onto reservations so that the new civilization could take whatever lands it deemed important.

The new government did not allow the Indians to have weapons of warfare and required them to rely on the government for sustenance. This caused a greater weakening of the American Indian spirit and way of life. The two greatest atrocities in terms of large scale deaths came next, the battle of Wounded Knee and the Trail of Tears.

The Trail of Tears happened in 1838 to 1839. It was the forced removal of the Cherokee tribes totaling approximately 17,000 Indians. Many of the peaceful tribes had established new lands and government in the Southeast after being driven from their lands by the encroaching white man's settlements. Despite this, all the Indians were rounded up, regardless of whether or not they were peaceful. Internment camps were set up, and they were rounded up and forced onto boats and then marched into the new Indian Territories.

It is estimated that around 4,000 Indians died from exposure, disease, and starvation during this forced trip. The Cherokee remembered this traditionally as "the trail where they cried" and today it is loosely translated and taught as The Trail of Tears.[3]

The Battle of Wounded Knee was so named to give it a semblance of honor for the American military when it was in fact a massacre that should have been prevented. It came about as a result of a movement called the Ghost Dance. This was a movement taught by a Paiute prophet named Wovoka who convinced the Sioux that if they followed certain rituals, the white man would disappear and the Indians would have their hunting lands and Buffalo back.

The movement became large enough among the reservation Indians that the Federal Government intervened. They attempted to arrest

Chief Sitting Bull but killed him instead. This caused fear among a large group of Sioux and they fled the reservation. Once off the reservation, even though they did not have weapons, the American Army classified them as hostiles and pursued them.

On December 28th, 1890 they were surrounded at Wounded Knee Creek. One young brave was found to have a rifle, and a fight broke out attempting to get it back. During the scuffle, a shot rang out and one soldier was hit. Immediately the other soldiers of the 7th Calvary fired into the huddled group of Indians killing many of them. Some had hidden war clubs and knives in blankets and they immediately pulled them out and began to defend themselves as best they could against the rifles.

To the credit of the brave Sioux fighting for their lives, they killed about 30 soldiers despite overwhelming odds and a lack of modern weapons. I can only imagine the bravery and courage that it took for so many warriors to charge soldiers who were shooting at them from horseback with merely a war-club or a knife. The impetus probably came from the certainty that they were being massacred and a desire to defend their women and children. The Army killed all the warriors and then proceeded to murder any remaining witnesses. 44 Women and 16 children were murdered and approximately 100 fighting age males (although that number may have been inflated to avoid listing many more children).[4]

Most of the events that led to the downfall of the Native American Nations before these two events were not the concerted effort of Americans, as it all happened before America even existed. The Native Americans fought an incoming invader who wanted their lands. They lost. If anyone is to be "blamed" for the destruction of the Indian culture it is the European nations responsible for the settlement of these new lands.

America should not be despised for rising up out of the ashes of the conflict. Blame the nations that started the conflict; France, England, and Spain. I contend, however; that no one is to blame. This is, and always has been, the way nations were built. There is not a single country in existence today that did not steal their current lands from other nations or warlords or tribes of people. All the way back to Genghis Khan, the Roman Empire, Aztecs, the Egyptians, and yes,

America; nations have been built and borders enforced by those with the desire and the military might to keep it. It is the way of humanity. It is not unique to America and America is not somehow the only nation to be responsible for the destruction of former nations.

No. America is actually unique in how it has responded to the descendants of those it conquered. Other nations enslaved and eventually killed off the conquered peoples. Some nations resorted to outright genocide to ensure that the native populations did not rise up in revolt. Other nations simply drove the indigenous populations out and had the strength to keep them out forever.

America chose to let the American Indians stay and to actually (out of guilt) pay them a small sum of money and supplies every year as some sort of restitution for conquering them. To this day, the American Federal Government pays hundreds of millions of dollars to over 500 different Native American tribal governments as restitution for injustices, for mineral rights, right of passage for oil lines, compensation for land taken, etc.

Meanwhile, the conquered people's descendants have formed organizations within the conquerors society that legally fight for money, land, and other compensations and special rights. No other nation on earth has allowed that to happen. Logically, this is a ridiculous thing for a nation to allow and it has done nothing but hurt the new nation's economy and society.

America has chosen to give the descendants of the conquered people permanent land to form their own nations within its own while also retaining the same rights of American citizenship. According to www.usa.gov/tribes:

> *"The U.S. government officially recognizes more than 500 Indian tribes in the contiguous 48 states and Alaska. These federally recognized tribes are eligible for funding and services from the Bureau of Indian Affairs, either directly or through contracts, grants, or compacts.*
>
> *...*
>
> *[the] Indian Trust Program—Consists of 55 million surface acres and 57 million acres of subsurface minerals estates held in trust by the United States for individual*

The contention that America doesn't pay anything to Native Americans is patently false. We continue to take money from every tax paying American and give a portion of it to each of the 562 federally recognized Indian tribal governments. These nations within a nation do not strengthen America; rather they harm America as a whole. This is not to say that the American Indian does not deserve citizenship at this point, it is just that the American nation does not deserve to continually and indefinitely pay "restitution" for something that was ultimately a natural and normal human cycle.

The American Indian spirit and history is a vital part of America's history and they deserve our respect and admiration for many things. The warrior spirit of many tribes has become the spirit of America's military and in fact, they taught us a lot of what we currently use as battle tactics. Also, American Indians have traditionally joined our military and fought in record numbers in every war that we have fought.

The Windtalkers of the Navajo nation helped us win World War II. The war cries, guerilla warfare, and stoic fighting spirit still carry on in our Marines to this day. At Fort Huachuca the Army has a museum that has many letters, quotes, and pictures from Indians who joined our military. One such warrior called the American Marines "the new American Indian" because he recognized the same fighting spirit and honor code that he was raised with as a young brave.

Conquering a nation (or in this case, many smaller nations) does not make a country inherently racist. America has actually done more than any other nation to try to rectify the injustices it did commit such as those at Wounded Knee and the Trail of Tears, but that has not made American's racist. In fact, it shows something entirely different. America has such a big heart and such a concern to right injustices that we are willing to self-flagellate our country out of guilt. We agonize over people that are long dead, what we should give their descendants, and how we should tell our children that our country is horrible because of what happened.

This type of action for an individual is similar to that of a teenager cutting themselves because they have a low self-esteem. It is not normal, it is not productive, it is self-destructive and should not be allowed. America needs to stop paying reparations for the sins of the past and move forward to help us become the great melting pot that we once were. Our politicians need to start being adults about things and stop thinking that we can make everything better by throwing money at the grandchildren and great grandchildren of those who suffered.

A simple way to end this would be to make a one-time payment of a large sum of money to each and every Indian still alive today, remove all payments to tribes and remove special rights, and put an amendment in the constitution that would not allow anymore reparations or payments to any of the conquered nations. America should allow each person to choose to swear loyalty to America or lose their citizenship. This is fair, this is normal, and this would be the rational thing to do.

America should come first, and cultural heritage that does not have first loyalty to this Sovereign country should come second. That heritage is something that should be taught in the home and not endorsed by this country. People should choose to be American first, not something else if they want to enjoy the benefits of this great nation.

We should be proud of what America has become and the contributions of the American Indian to our society. The world is by far better off due to America. The spirit of freedom and the warrior spirit that we assimilated from the American Indian have enabled us to fight for freedom around the globe and win two world wars.

In some tribes, their fighting spirit was balanced by their spirituality and oneness with nature. The pioneers respected and envied the Indians for their knowledge of nature, medicines, hunting, and surviving with nature, oftentimes in an environment that would kill a normal person. This balance between love of nature, the noble warrior, and yes even the bloody savage will always be a part of America's spirit and heritage. This is something that every American should teach their children about regardless of the color of their skin.

Irish

Beginning in 1845 the potato blight that struck Europe hit Ireland the harshest. Due to political and economic conditions, the Irish were dependent upon the potato as their staple diet. The blight caused a famine that lasted approximately seven years. During that time, almost a quarter of the population fled the country, most of them to America. Hoping for food, opportunity, and a fresh start in life, almost 2 million Irish landed on the shores of America. This was probably the greatest migration of the 19th Century.[5]

Many Irish were forced to migrate for various reasons. Some were indentured servants. Some were tenants who could no longer afford rent. Some were escaping starvation with their last dime. Some were prisoners, some were debtors, and some were forced into it. Regardless, very few if any, did it because they wanted to and had the choice. America was a chance at a new life, and for many, the possibility of life itself.

Unfortunately, the reality was very grim. It is estimated that as many as one quarter of the Irish died on the journey. Disease, filth, cramped conditions, and starvation killed untold thousands on their way across the ocean. The boats were often as bad as slave conditions for various reasons. The lack of money to purchase good lodging, the fact that the Irish were viewed as peasants and servant class people at best, and many times the mere fact that nobody cared once they were on the ships. Once they made it to America…if they made it to America, things weren't much better.

The Irish were hated for several reasons. The first, which is probably true for many immigrants and in many countries, was that they were immigrants. Previous groups of immigrants looked at them as outsiders and a threat to what they had worked for. It was the same for the first waves of Europeans that came after the pioneers had struggled to survive in the new land. These newcomers had not built anything, they didn't know the struggles the previous people faced, and they wanted land and jobs. Who were they going to take it from? That was the common fear and still is to this day whenever a new wave of immigrants goes anywhere.

The second reason they were hated was because they were typically Catholic. America was started by people literally fleeing that state religion. When the Irish came and wanted to build Catholic churches and literally bring that religion with them, it was an affront to most Americans at the time. This was a mere 60 years or so after America won her freedom from Great Britain. There were still many alive who had actually fought in that war and many more who grew up on the stories of the atrocities of the King and why America was founded.

It quickly became socially acceptable to discriminate against the Irish. Newspapers and magazines regularly depicted the Irish in caricatures making fun of them and calling them all sorts of names. The common view of the Irish was that they were dirty, rowdy, unchristian, illiterate, incapable, and just plain undesirable. Employers refused to hire the Irish. In fact, this systematic discrimination was so prevalent that the word NINA was often scrawled on help wanted signs and everyone knew that it meant "No Irish Need Apply".

It seemed that the only jobs the Irish could get were the dangerous and difficult jobs that others were not willing to take for the cheap pay that was offered. These immigrants were used by those in industry to make the business owners rich. Thousands of Irish died to build America's infrastructure and there were many people to blame. Our lax immigration laws allowed poor immigrants to flow in by the hundreds of thousands. These poor people were willing to work for anything because they needed food. Business owners took advantage and hired these immigrants that nobody cared about, at low wages, and without thought to their safety. Irish workers slaved over the building of America's canals and railroads etc. in many times hazardous and life-threatening conditions that others would not put up with. It was that, or starve.

In the South, slave owners would not dare risk the loss of their "expensive property" so oftentimes these dangerous jobs would go to the Irish. Without any protection such as labor unions, minimum wage laws, or safety regulations, many workers died on the job and it was just considered normal.

Not only were the Irish discriminated against economically by way of the workforce, but it was also political and social. Ethnic street gangs clashed and often ended up in mob fights. Irish, German, and blacks were often pitted against each other. They were all competing for a higher standing on the socio-economic ladder.

The Democrat party saw an opportunity to buy votes and they appointed "ward bosses" to garner the Irish vote. These bosses were the mediators between the political party and the constituents that they promised favors to if they voted Democrat. Many Irish became Democrats in return for these promises while blacks tended to vote Republican due to the principles and platform of that party. The racial tensions escalated with each of these stark differences in ideology. This exacerbated the racial differences at the voting booths and elsewhere.

Additionally, a "Nativist" party was formed in America specifically to combat politically the influx of Catholics and immigrants. During the 40s and 50s this party came to power based on its opposition to immigration. It did not have much of a platform other than to block immigration and to prevent Catholics from obtaining elected positions. Its followers typically replied that they "know nothing" about the activities and ideals of the party. They largely succeeded in electing governors and mayors of cities and as a result the open discrimination of the Irish continued for some time.[6]

The Irish spirit prevailed over time. They banded together and began to form labor unions to make things better on the job and to demand better pay. These labor unions ultimately served to better conditions for all Americans and led to reforms in work safety, regulations, and pay. They formed alliances and became a strong enough voice that they were able to elect politicians that favored them.

Towards the end of the 19th century things had improved. By the 20th century, things were vastly better for the Irish politically and socially. Due to continued immigration, persistence, and hard work, they finally had enough numbers to sway public and political opinion. Their contributions to society and America as a whole because of these things earned them a reputation for having an unbeatable spirit and had finally earned them a place in America's history books.

In modern history, Congress proclaimed March as Irish-American Heritage Month in 1995. By 2009 36.9 million Americans claimed Irish heritage of which 92% had finished high school. This is compared to the national average of only 85% of Americans finishing high school. Also, the Irish as a whole had finally risen above the "poor" stereotype and through hard work had attained a median household income of roughly $56,000 compared to the national median income of $50,221. Despite the past, or maybe because of it, the Irish have "pulled themselves up by their own bootstraps" and overcome the discrimination they previously faced in America.[7]

Asian

The racism against Asians in America came in varied forms at different times. The migration of people's from Asian countries came in waves depending on which country and also primarily on the need for laborers in America. Without going into detail on the economic reasons of their respective countries, it is sufficient to say that America offered a chance at economic security and a new start in a country that promised freedom and hope to the world. They came from many places including Korea, Vietnam, Japan, China, the Philippines and other countries.

Like every other great immigrant wave in virtually every country and time period around the world, problems arose. The simple economic reality is that whenever a large group of people immigrate to a new country, they almost never have homes or jobs waiting for them. The result is that hunger, homelessness, and desperation cause these immigrants to be willing to work any job just so that they can survive. This creates a workforce that is willing to make concessions in pay, type of labor, safety, and benefits merely to be able to have a job. It should come as no surprise then that the new workers take more dangerous jobs for lower pay than the previous workers were willing to do.

Employers are almost always in business to make money, so it makes sense to higher workers at less pay and to reduce overhead by cutting standards, safety, and benefits. The thousands of desperate workers naturally take the work because any money is better than none, and both parties are relieved at the mutually agreed upon labor. This drives down wages and the other companies that were paying more to the previous workers now are making less of a profit due to their labor costs. Pay cuts or outright firing results in less high paid workers and more openings for the new lower wage immigrants. This naturally creates volatile situations between the old workforce and the new.

When the new immigrant work force happens to be of a different race or nationality, it makes it easy to discriminate because those new immigrants who are taking the jobs are readily identifiable. While this is wrong, the logic is undeniable. It has happened all over the world in every developing nation that offers opportunity. America was no different.

In 1848 news of the discovery of gold in California started the great Gold Rush that lasted almost seven years. People from all over the world came to California in the hopes of becoming rich. This began a great migration from China and it continued for several years even after the California Gold Rush. Chinese laborers took jobs in the coal mines initially but became instrumental in many other fields as well. The construction of the Intercontinental railroad took advantage of the influx of cheap labor, as well as several other industries like Textiles, service industries such as laundry and food service, and agriculture.

The term "Coolie" is often used to refer to Chinese laborers during this time period but it is really a British term that merely means laborer. Many of these laborers were in fact indentured servants that had a contract of 5-7 years or so, but they oftentimes did not live to fulfill their contracts due to harsh labor conditions.

These new immigrants didn't just face poor labor conditions; they also faced anti-Chinese sentiment which grew quickly. It is no coincidence that this sentiment grew at a rate proportional to the rate of immigration and jobs lost to these new low paid and hard-working foreigners. There were several riots and mob led attacks during this time that intentionally led to the deaths of many Chinese. The "Chinese Massacre of 1871" and the "Snake River Massacre" are two of the most notable ones. Like with every period of racism, there are many individual atrocities and stories that society turned a blind eye to, if not directly permitted.

The state of California began passing laws specifically aimed at discrimination of the

Chinese. Taxes on Chinese business, limitations to the number of Chinese people allowed on immigration vessels coming into the state, and even special licensing requirements for Chinese owned business were all laws passed by California that were later ruled to be violations of federal law.

In addition to state laws, a major Federal law against the Chinese was enacted as well. In 1882 President Rutherford B. Hayes was able to get Congress to pass the Chinese Exclusion Act which terminated Chinese immigration for ten years. This act was reinstated several times over the next few decades until wording was put in to make it indefinite. It wasn't until 1943 that the Chinese Exclusion Acts were repealed by Congress.[8]

The Chinese labor force was often mistreated, but as with previous immigrant groups, they overcame their difficulties. Many laborers saw the opportunity in less desirable jobs such as laundry services and actually built their own businesses and became successful in their own right due to their entrepreneurial spirit. The Chinese, like so many immigrant groups before them, had to learn to stick together because they were despised, looked down upon, and rejected by society at large.

As a result, China towns sprang up wherever there were large groups of Chinese immigrants. They are still thriving to this day in many large cities around America and the achievements of the previous immigrants have led to many great things in this country. Labor reforms, rights of land and business ownership, and the great advances that the Intercontinental Railroad made possible were all part of their contributions to the great Melting Pot of American society.

After the Chinese Exclusion Acts, cheap labor had to come from somewhere else for large plantation owners in Hawaii. From 1903 to 1905 some 7,000 Korean laborers were recruited and shortly afterwards over 1,100 "picture brides" were brought in. These brides were similar to the mail-order brides of the American Wild West. Hard-working men made the difficult journey and struggled to survive in the new world. Those that did survive yearned for families after carving out a living. They advertised for women back home to come out to marry a man who was established with a home and a job. Due to immigration laws, many of these women had to be married before setting foot in Hawaii. They were called "picture brides" because they would be married on the boats with merely a picture of the groom that they were about to meet.

Another wave of Korean immigration happened after America's involvement in the Korean War in the 1950s. This was in large part the result of American soldiers marrying and adopting children and bringing them back to America after the war. It wasn't until 1965 that Koreans were able to apply for permanent resident status in America.[9] The Immigration and Naturalization Act of 1965, also known as the Hart-Celler Act, brought a great change to America's immigration. It recognized the humanity of immigrants regardless of race. Rather than a quota system based on country, this act allowed immigrant families to join their relatives and also allowed for skilled laborers to come based upon the needs of the American labor force. This Act still placed a cap on immigration but it was based upon the principles of the Civil Rights movement and allowed freer immigration especially from Asian, African, and Latin America countries.[10]

Probably the greatest instance of racism against Asians in America was the Japanese internment camps after the bombing of Pearl Harbor in 1941. On December 7th, 1941 Japanese fighter planes attacked the U.S. Naval base at Pearl Harbor destroying 18 ships, over 160 aircraft, and killing over 2,400 American servicemen. December 8th, the United States as well as its ally Great Britain, declared war on Japan. Within days of that tragedy, the FBI director assured the Attorney General that all suspects were already in custody with regard to possible Japanese sympathizers. Unfortunately the discussion had already begun about rounding up all those of Japanese descent.

Lt. Gen. John L. DeWitt, head of the Western Defense Command, pushed his racially charged agenda believing that "the Japanese race is an enemy race". He stated that, "while many second and third generation Japanese born on United States soil, possessed of United States citizenship, have become 'Americanized,' the racial strains are undiluted." [11] With his help, and the push by several congressmen to move all those of Japanese descent into concentration camps, political pressure was put on the President to do something. Even the head of the California

Grower-Shipper Vegetable Association told the Saturday Evening Post:

"If all of the Japs were removed tomorrow, we'd never miss them… because the white farmers can take over and produce everything the Jap grows. And we don't want them back when the war ends, either." [11]

This sentiment and political pressure helped create Executive Order 9066 that President Roosevelt signed in February 1942 just over two months after the attack. This order allowed the war department to designate "military areas" and then remove all who it felt to be a danger to America from that area. It was specifically aimed at the Japanese population even though several thousand Germans and Italians as well as other Asians were rounded up. More than 110,000 Japanese and Japanese-Americans were rounded up and taken to impromptu internment camps in ten different locations. On April 30th, that year, notices were posted up and down the West coast informing those of Japanese descent (up to 1/16th Japanese blood) that they had exactly one week to get their affairs in order for relocation.[11]

Many Japanese farmers, business owners, and homeowners lost everything due to not being able to sell or being forced to sell for whatever they could get. Many greedy people eagerly snapped up possessions and land at rock-bottom prices without concern for what was happening to the Japanese Americans. Almost nobody spoke out. One woman, Emily Stephany, remembers her school friends saying goodbye and never seeing them again.[53] Neighbors, friends, and co-workers disappeared and most Americans failed to speak out or even protest a single word. One survivor and American citizen Robert Kashiwagi remembers it vividly. [11]

> *"As far as I'm concerned, I was born here, and according to the Constitution that I studied in school, that I had the Bill of Rights that should have backed me up. And until the very minute I got onto the evacuation train, I says, 'It can't be'. I says, 'How can they do that to an American citizen?'"*

The camps were poorly managed and were basically secure prisons hastily built in the middle of nowhere with armed guards. The Japanese-Americans were allowed a bit more freedom than regular prisons and even organized schools, shops, baseball leagues, etc. in order to try and maintain a sense of a normal community. Those that tried to escape were still shot and the ever present armed guards made it next to impossible to escape that reality.

After WWII the anti-Japanese sentiment began to diminish in America for two main reasons. One, the public knowledge of what the Nazi's did in the concentration camps, mainly for racial reasons, opened up the eyes of the general public to the horrors of racism. Two, in 1943 the U.S. government authorized those of Japanese descent to join the military and fight. This resulted in the formation of the Japanese American 442nd Regimental Combat Team. Their heroics and decorations for bravery and valor in combat became widely known and helped many Americans to change their views of Asian-Americans.

In 1945 the remaining detainees were released, most with nothing to their name. Some attempted to return home to find their houses occupied and had to fight to get evictions just to get their property back. Many had to start over. In 1948 the Federal Government issued partial reparations to some Japanese Americans, and in 1970 President Gerald R. Ford finally rescinded Executive Order 9066. It wasn't until some 40 years later that the government issued an official apology. Finally, in 1988 under President Ronald Reagan, the Civil Liberties Act was signed, and each surviving detainee was issued an official apology letter along with $20,000. [12]

One survivor put it this way: *"The government made a mistake, and they apologized,"* Asako Tokuno said. *"Made redress. And tried to make things right. You can't eliminate all the feelings and the hurts that happened, but the fact that, what other country would do so ... do that? I kind of wonder. So, there are a lot of great things about our country. And I don't think I'd ever want to live anywhere else."* [11]

<u>Hispanic</u>

The history of Mexican assimilation and discrimination in the United States of America can be summed up in a few paragraphs. The main difference between them and previously discussed racial groups that were discriminated against was that Mexicans did not so much immigrate into America as much as they have always been a part of America. The western frontier, before it was settled and broken into states that were claimed by or bought by the U.S.A., was largely wild and controlled by various Indian tribes. The towns or ranches that did exist in the southwestern part of the country were usually Mexican, considering that a large part of the west was recognized as owned by Mexico.

Gradually Americans pushed west and began settling in what was then Mexico. These [mostly] white people integrated with the Mexicans in society, business and land dealings, and for entertainment. American western culture was greatly influenced by Latinos because their culture was our culture. Many American cowboys and ranchers learned their trade from the great Mexican Caballeros or Mexican Cowboys. The term Caballero is generally translated as gentleman but was more widely used in the Western frontier to mean cowboy. The terms lariat, or lasso, and many other common western terms and phrases came from the Spanish language and were used as a normal part of the American westerner's language.

Mexican parties, music, dances, and food were all part of the everyday and common life of many western towns. The culture was synonymous with the American Wild West. Many westerners greatly respected the Mexican culture and even valued their expertise. This is not to say that discrimination did not happen, merely that those who lived in the West generally respected them. As towns grew and Easterners pushed into the West, the two cultures clashed. This led to racism and discrimination on both sides. This had more to do with the western culture of cowboys, ranches, and the reliance on guns than it did with race.

As towns and industry grew and relied less on the ranches for income and life itself, the Americans began to push out and exclude those who still lived the simple life outside of cities. This didn't merely exclude Mexicans, but also any who were viewed as backward, uncouth, or wild people who lived outside the towns and off the land. Unless someone was a wealthy and well known rancher, the respect for people of the Wild West was short lived. Laws were made against cowboys entering town with weapons, raucous drinking and partying etc. Civilization came to the towns at the same time that discrimination came against those who had settled those very towns.

This is actually true of almost every country and culture that has ever existed. It takes wild and courageous men/women to tame a land. As soon as towns spring up, those warriors and brave adventurous people are often barred from the new society that they helped create. "Civilized" people are often afraid of the wild people that made their towns possible. The freedoms and luxury that exist in civilized towns would not be possible without those people who came before, and yet; they are ridiculed, discriminated against, and thrust out as lepers.

Often, this resulted in de facto discrimination against Mexicans that were viewed as the same cut of cloth as American cowboys or vice versa. However, there was no Federal or governmental institutionalized racism against Mexicans in the United States. There was no concerted effort against Hispanics in America like there was against the Irish, Chinese, and Blacks, etc. The intertwined histories, families, lifestyle, and hardships of Mexicans and Americans are the reason. The everyday American understood and co-existed with Mexicans. This is not to say that towns and groups of people did not discriminate based on race, just that it was not a far reaching American phenomenon.

In 1821 Mexico gained Independence from Spain and contracted with America to bring in settlers along the Brazos River to help tame their land. The settlers received money and land on the condition that they would:

1. Be loyal to the Mexican government
2. Learn the Spanish language
3. Convert to Roman Catholicism

These settlers, brought in by the Mexican government brought with them the American ideas of Independence and freedom from oppressive governments. When Santa Ana became dictator of Mexico in 1834 he sought to crush the independent spirit of these settlers and the Mexican communities and cities that dared to defy him. In October 1835 he sent the Army to Gonzalez to take away the cannon that was defending the town from Indians. These Texans fired the cannon on the Mexican army and later took it to the Alamo to defend the people there. The skirmish at Gonzalez became known as the first battle for Texas Independence.[13]

This is also the town that started the very American idea that no one can take our guns from us unless from our cold dead hands. The flag they hoisted over the town had a picture of the cannon and the words "Come and take it". The phrase goes all the way back to that of the Spartans who uttered the same thing against King Xerxes I over 2000 years prior, "Molon Labe" in Greek.[14]

On April 21st, 1836 Texas gained Independence from Mexico and all former Mexicans that stayed became Texans. December 29th, 1845 Texas became the 28th state to join America. The end result is that many people of Mexican descent and even some who had lived as Mexicans became Americans in the early beginnings of the United States. Their culture and rich heritage is actually part of America and not separate. Those Mexicans that chose to rise up against their own government to form the Republic of Texas actually had more American spirit than Mexican. Their independence FROM Mexico was intentionally sought and won. They chose to become American and America became better for it.

Those Mexicans who choose to immigrate to America today and yet want to retain the Mexican flag and march against our flag, have truly forgotten their history. Those Americans of Mexican descent who now try to change history and cry about Hispanic/Latino discrimination in the United States should simply forfeit their U.S.A. citizenship and go to Mexico if they truly believe it is better.

America did not steal Texas from Mexico; Mexicans rose up and fought against Mexico so that they could become free. Later, they asked to become part of America.

Let us not forget history and those Mexicans who fought and bled and died to escape their home country. They earned the right to be called Americans, and their descendants are spitting in their faces.

<u>Blacks</u>

There is no doubt that blacks have been discriminated against in the United States of America. Anyone who says otherwise has obviously not picked up a history book or been paying attention their whole life. Racism has not always been a part of American history, but slavery certainly opened that door and kept it at the forefront of our culture for some time. In parts of the country, especially Western American culture where one's character was infinitely more important, racism did not flourish until later. For instance, ranchers, gold miners and the like that had to rely on the character of those around them for life itself (courage to fight Indians, work ethic to survive in the wilderness, ability to bind a wound and willingness to help others etc.) often did not care about skin color. As civilization took hold and people had the luxury of towns and relative safety, they also were physically able to discriminate without fear of losing their life.

Slavery is a human condition and character flaw that has been around since the dawn of time. Groups of people who found themselves stronger than others have slaughtered those weaker and taken slaves on every continent. This is not an American phenomenon. Slavery has been the bane of human existence on every continent in almost every culture and without exception, every race throughout history. The reason it is such a sore subject in America is because we are a relatively new nation and it happened so recently in our history. Also, many people make money off of keeping racism alive.   Yet, there are currently estimates of 160 modern countries that still have some form of slavery and at least 15 of those countries legally allow it. Among those 15 are China, Russia, North Korea, India, Congo, Pakistan, Iraq, and Indonesia. It is estimated that approximately 46 million people currently live in slavery around the world.[15]

The first Black slaves were brought to America in 1619 by the Europeans. Remember that America was not a nation until they rose up against their English tyrant in 1776, which was well over 150 years after slavery was already established on this land. The tobacco crops and later the cotton crops of the new world were ripe for the abuses of the slave trade. A new world, away from the eyes of civilization where slavery could be practiced and people could be taken advantage of without the rule of law, was easy pickings for the rich and powerful of Europe. Land was for the taking as were people who could be abused without the threat of a nation or army to defend them.

Slavery was an established fact on this continent when the common people finally rose up against the King of England and wrote the Declaration of Independence. It was an unfortunate part of life in society and the economy when the colonies began the Revolutionary War. The Declaration of Independence and the Constitution of the United States of America could not conceivably address the issue of slavery (although we will discuss some of the words used pertaining to that later in this book). The legal issue would come later for this new nation, but first, they had to establish that they were a nation so that they could begin making their own laws.

The Colonies revolted against the tyrant king and it took a drastic toll on resources, the land, and all people that lived here. They won their freedom and formed the new nation with a new type of government, a Democratic Republic. It was the first nation of its kind in recorded history and they were about to make history again with this issue of slavery.

The slaves in America were treated as slaves have always been treated in human history. They were treated worse than cattle as they were shipped in by the thousands from their traffickers in Africa. Everyone knows the history, or should by now. Warring tribes in Africa saw profit and power in the genocide and enslavement of their neighbors. They sold each other to the Europeans, pirates, and profiteers all over the world. Thousands died in the inhuman conditions on the boats and who knows how many thousands died in the battles to procure them. Once they reached the shores of each country, they were paraded in front of buyers, sold like animals, and lived out their lives with endless degradation and lack of humanity.

Slavery is never pretty, and in America it was no better than anywhere else… at first. Some owners bought slaves to breed them and sell their children. Some bought slaves merely because they were sadistic and wanted people to beat, rape, and kill legally. The majority bought slaves for cheap labor, merely to be used like farm equipment and killed when they were no longer useful. However, a few Americans actually bought slaves to save them. Similar to what has happened all over the world at various times and places, when someone of a good heart with a moral conscience sees evil, they try to stop it. There is record of some Americans looking to buy entire families just to try to keep them together. Some were bought to actually treat them as humans so that they could avoid the life that another not so well intentioned master would inflict on them.

Blacks were not allowed to learn to read or write and were often beaten if found attempting it. Some masters actually taught their slaves in secret because they saw the injustice of it. One story is that of a woman from Texas. I personally know her descendant who owns a barbecue restaurant in Albuquerque New Mexico. Her master treated her well because she knew how to cook. He threw the best lawn parties around and she made a name for herself because of her famous barbecues. She had a better life living as a slave in his house than she would have been able to have in that time period anywhere else in America (this is a testament to good people, NOT giving credence to the Democrat cry that slavery was better for black people than freedom). Her recipe was passed down over the generations and with a few modifications her family has been able to make a successful business that still thrives to this day. While that is a single anecdote in the misery of the slave trade, it was not so uncommon as to be the only one. A simple internet search will show many such stories.

The issue of slavery in America became repugnant to many very quickly due to the core values of freedom, personal property, and individuality that caused the colonies to overthrow the King of England. America was split on the issue, to such an extent that laws were made in various states that were diametrically opposed to each other. Some made laws to specifically encourage slavery, promote it, and punish any person who helped a slave escape. Other states made laws that specifically outlawed slavery and punished those who attempted to recapture a slave that had escaped to that state.

The Underground Railroad was formed in the early 1800s and was a secret network of people who helped slaves escape. There were many routes and many people, mostly white, who were known as stationmasters or conductors. These people had homes, churches, etc. that had hiding places where escaped slaves could find refuge before being guided carefully to the next "station" until they were far enough north that they could be free. Canada already allowed blacks the same freedom as whites and it is thought that some of the Underground Railroad was based in that country.

Many former slaves made it their life's work to help other slaves escape. Two of the most well-known are Harriet Tubman and Frederick Douglass. Harriet Tubman went so far as to go back to her previous slave home to help her husband escape. He had remarried and refused to go with her, attesting to the fact that not all slave owners were vile inhuman creatures. She regularly took her escapees to Canada to avoid American society entirely.

Frederick Douglass was also a former slave who lived in Rochester New York and he was able to document at least 400 slaves that he personally helped.[16] An innumerable amount of people helped, and well over 40,000 slaves were able to escape to the Northern free states and to Canada. This movement helped change the climate in America against slavery to the one that led to the Civil War.

In 1854 the anti-slavery Whigs (political party of the time) got together and formed the Republican Party specifically to see the end of the legal slave trade that they abhorred. In 1860, the Republican Party ran a candidate by the name of Abraham Lincoln. The 8th and 9th point in his political platform was this:

__8__. That the normal condition of all the territory of the United States is that of freedom: That, as our Republican fathers, when they had abolished slavery in all our national territory, ordained that "no persons should be deprived of life, liberty or property without due process of law," it becomes our duty, by legislation, whenever such legislation is necessary, to maintain this provision of the Constitution against all attempts to violate it; and we deny the authority of Congress, of a territorial legislature, or of any individuals, to give legal existence to slavery in any territory of the United States.

__9__. That we brand the recent reopening of the African slave trade, under the cover of our national flag, aided by perversions of judicial power, as a crime against humanity and a burning shame to our country and age; and we call upon Congress to take prompt and efficient measures for the total and final suppression of that execrable traffic[17]

Abraham Lincoln won the Presidency on Nov. 6th, 1860 and within twelve weeks, six states succeeded from the Union out of fear that the new President would take away their slaves and thus a major source of labor and income. In April 1861 the new Confederacy declared war by attacking Fort Sumter in South Carolina. The Civil War was about secession and the rights of states over the Federal government, but the secession was 100% about slavery.

The end result was that the North won the war and slavery was abolished. The Emancipation Proclamation took effect on Jan. 1, 1863 and freed the slaves from most states and in 1865 the 13th amendment was adopted which freed them all. The 13th amendment states:

SECTION 1

Neither slavery nor involuntary servitude, except as a punishment for crime whereof the party shall have been duly convicted, shall exist within the United States, or any place subject to their jurisdiction.

SECTION 2

Congress shall have power to enforce this article by appropriate legislation.

Black people still struggled in America even after the 14th amendment, which granted citizenship to all those born in America; and finally, the 15th amendment which gave Blacks the right to vote in 1870. Jim Crow laws were passed in many states after the 15th amendment to force segregation upon Americans and the term "separate but equal" became commonplace. This idea was meant to make people feel good about their racial prejudice and discrimination because then they could say that they weren't depriving black people of anything because they were still "equal", merely "separate".

Unfortunately, or maybe fortunately for it led to the Civil Rights movement; this separate but equal mentality just allowed the racial prejudice and discrimination to ferment in our country for a very long time. It wasn't until 1954 that racial segregation in public schools was declared unconstitutional in the case of Brown vs. Board of Education in Topeka.[18] This sparked a rash of similar cases and laws that overturned Jim

Crow laws around the country and led to the Civil Rights Movement.

The Civil Rights Act of 1964 outlawed discrimination based on race, color, religion, sex, or national origin. Dr. Martin Luther King Jr. was instrumental in getting this passed and he was probably one of the most vocal leaders of the movement. However, proof of the hatred and racism that existed against blacks was his assassination on April 4th, 1968.

Another major form of discrimination came with the establishment of a group that called themselves the Ku Klux Klan (KKK) in 1866. They were basically the enforcement arm of the Democrat Party and their primary purpose was the opposition of the new anti-slavery Republican Party. They were an outright terrorist organization that used masks, fire, torture, and death to try to achieve their goal: that of keeping Black people as subhuman in our society. They directly attacked blacks all over the country and targeted Republican leaders whether white or black. Democrats sought to elect KKK members and in the South were able to succeed with the election of law enforcement officials, mayors of cities, and even members of Congress.

The Klan was purported to be over 5 million strong in its heyday and was a strong force in electing Democrats and preventing blacks from voting. Robert Byrd was elected as a Democrat Senator in 1959 and served until his death in 2010. He is famous for his attempt at stopping the Civil Rights Act of 1964 with a filibuster as well as his time in the Klan as Exalted Cyclops and Kleagle. There are many despicable quotes from this man and here is one from a letter he wrote to Senator Bilbo asserting that integration of the military was a huge mistake, and that he would rather:

> *"...die a thousand times, and see Old Glory trampled in the dirt never to rise again, than to see this beloved land of ours become degraded by race mongrels, a throwback to the blackest specimen from the wilds."* [19]

The fact that Senator Byrd was undefeated until 2010 when he died, just goes to show that either the entire Democrat Party has not had a problem with electing an open racist or they were completely ignorant of who they were electing. The reason this is so astonishing is two-fold.

One, Wikipedia states that nearly 31% of Americans identify themselves as Democrats. Two, according to factcheck.org all the way until 2004 nearly 88% of Black Americans voted Democrat.

The point is simply this: racism against Blacks has been pervasive across America in our society and even up to the top of our political structure in the Democrat Party. It wasn't until 1964, a relatively short time ago, that Blacks had legal authority to challenge any discrimination that they faced in society.

Nobody can legislate morality. People will always have their own ideas, even bad ones, and nobody can stop that. Racism on an individual basis will always exist. The best a society can do is to punish someone who openly expresses that racism. America finally reached that point in 1964 and over the following two or three decades was able to change societal mores and customs to the point that we no longer accept it. Criminals and evil people will always spring up for various reasons. What a society chooses to do with these people is what defines the morality of that society. America finally chose to do the right thing in 1964 with regard to racism.

While individual instances of racism still happens in every country and against every race (like the election of Klansman Byrd), the legal, societal, and institutionalized racism of America's past has finally ended. It is no longer accepted or allowed in America. The mere charge of racism, even without proof, is enough to end careers in America today.

The greatest proof that American society as a whole finally accepted Blacks as equals happened in 2008. On Nov 6, 2008 a black man, Barack Hussein Obama was elected to the most powerful position in the entire free world, the President of the United States of America. He will forever go down in history as the first black man to become President in America. Not only that, but he was elected again in 2012. No country that is racist against Blacks would ever elect a Black President to have power over them. Americans proved that a black person could truly become anything they wanted in America and the color of their skin would not stop them.

Obama ran his campaign with the slogans of "Change we can believe in" and "Hope". He promised to fundamentally change America and give hope for the future. His election to the highest office in the land was supposed to signal a turn away from racism and a better future for not just Black Americans but for all Americans. Throughout his Presidency Barack Obama constantly brought up the issues of race relations in America and he did indeed affect a change because of that.

Chapter 3 Racism: Where it Comes From and What it Leads to

All one has to do to see where racism comes from is to talk to the parent of a racist person. People who truly believe in racism have no problem openly sharing their reasoning. Parents teach children their values, and racists are no different. Many young children are brought up to believe racism is natural or justified.

When a child grows up and develops their mind and their own thoughts and reasons, that is when core values and a worldview are developed. This usually happens during the adolescent years when a child becomes a bit rebellious against their parents and other authority. What is taught prior to that will have a great influence on a child determining their own value system, but it can be overcome if the individual is strong willed enough or truly seeks answers.

It is not enough to know what you believe. An introspective person will seek to find out **why** they believe something. Yes, racism is taught, but adults most often have a different reason for why they are still racist.

Religion, politics, personal experience, and even logic and science can all be deciding factors in an adult's choice to be racist. Whatever the reason, the individual makes a personal choice to follow this path and it becomes a major part of their worldview. A worldview is a particular philosophy or perspective on the world around you. A worldview is like a pair of glasses with colored lenses. Everything you view is colored by that particular philosophy. Someone who has a worldview that everyone is basically good and that everything always turns out okay in the end is considered to be viewing the world through "rose-colored glasses" because they think everything will always turn out rosy.

Changing your worldview, once it is established, is a life changing event. It requires two things to happen. First, one must come face to face with a harsh reality that directly opposes your worldview. Secondly, you must choose to accept that reality and change your worldview based on the new evidence. Most people are not strong enough to change their worldview once it is established; they would rather ignore the reality. This produces cognitive dissonance which allows someone to function with a completely wrong or ignorant point of view. These types of people cannot be reasoned with because they have already chosen to ignore facts or reality.

Racism Caused by Religion

Religion is most often responsible for setting firm foundations in people's philosophy of life. For instance, anyone who reads the Christian Holy Bible will quickly find that Jesus valued individual life over the collective whole. Christians are taught that life is sacred because God created man and woman in His image. This worldview leads to a value of the individual above all else. This was ingrained in America's founding and in our military.

The Declaration of Independence states

> *"We hold these truths to be self-evident, that all men are created equal, that they are endowed by their Creator with certain unalienable rights that among these are life, liberty and the pursuit of happiness."*

This came from a religious belief in a God who created man in his image. This value of human life changed forever the way warfare was fought. In most of human history, Generals and political leaders used soldiers as mere pawns and cannon fodder because they did not care about the individual soldier. Often in the past, soldiers were conscripts or slaves. America changed this view of battles by valuing the lives of their soldiers and having a purely volunteer army.

We learned to fight like the Indians, to make every soldiers life count by fighting from behind shelter, using guerilla warfare tactics, and sometimes even running away instead of foolishly dying to prove a point. Soldiers are asked to go on suicide missions, very rarely are they ordered to do so. It is why the American soldier has the creed of "No man left behind". It is why six soldiers died on missions searching for one missing soldier, Bowe Bergdahl in 2009, even though those soldiers knew that he was a deserter.[21]

This worldview is one of the reasons that America's military has become a world power to be feared. Every soldier knows that his life is valuable and that the entire military might of our great nation is behind him. This ideology is not taught in the military (for the most part), but it is ingrained in the institution because it was founded for a noble purpose by a nation founded on the Christian religion. When I was in training with the Marines, we commonly heard the name of Jesus Christ used, and not always as an expletive. We were told that the only time we didn't snap to attention when an officer entered the room was when the Chaplain was there. The Chaplain was a representative of God Himself and thus had a higher rank than any other officer.

Every night of my training, we were told to line up in the barracks. At the command, "Pray", we were to bow our heads to reflect on the day or pray to the god of our choice. These practices have obviously been watered down over the years to allow for different religions and those of no religion to do as they wish, but the point is simply that our military had a strong religious background.

That being said, there are some religious people who attempt to use the Bible to justify their racism. Some have said that the story of Cain killing Abel (in the book of Genesis) shows

God's judgement on Cain and all his descendants by putting a "mark" on Cain that was literally a changing of his skin color. Nowhere in any Biblical text does this mark indicate a changing of skin color let alone saying what color it supposedly was. However, there were some churches and individuals that firmly believed God marked his skin black and that all black people were his descendants and deserved to be looked down upon. Never mind that the Bible teaches equality and never mentions skin color as a reason for anything. In fact, the Bible clearly states that God looks on the heart, not the outward appearance of men.

Some people have even used the tower of Babel story in Genesis chapter 11 to justify their racism. That is a story of how the people of the world rebelled against God and came together to build a tower to heaven. God confused their languages in the story and the rebellion came to a halt because people couldn't understand each other. Eventually, the people formed into groups of people that could understand each other and they all left the tower and went off into their own regions of the world.

Some people who call themselves Christian use this story to separate language groups and skin color and justify their racism or xenophobia (fear of people from other countries) by saying that God doesn't want people to associate with those of other language groups. This is again a clear misrepresentation of the story and what the Bible teaches about rebelling against God. Also, the story says nothing about skin color. In other places, the Bible advocates learning other languages and even Jesus Himself spoke at least two languages (Hebrew and Koine Greek) and possibly Aramaic as well.

There may be other religions that actually do advocate racism, but without a doubt people do use religion to push whatever ideology they choose to subscribe to. It doesn't matter if the religion itself teaches something or not, people have always twisted religion to suit their means. Having a "GOD" behind you supporting your belief system makes people feel better about themselves and often makes their worldview unshakeable. Most people have come across some religious person at some point in their life who refuses to accept reality because their god is above it all and "the rest of the world just doesn't understand". A religious drive behind any ideology can be the impetus someone needs to risk their life for a cause, or to take a life.

This is not always a bad thing as most religions teach people morality and how to be good individuals. When religion is used to push people to believe something evil, like racism, it becomes a problem. It is always hard to fight against an idea, but it is harder to fight when it is someone's religion driving them.

Racism Caused by Politics

Politics is another reason that some people have chosen to be racist. In American politics in the early 1800's the Democrat party chose to be racist in order to gain and keep political power. The Democrat party united under Andrew Jackson in 1824 and called themselves Jacksonian Democrats. The Whig Party was formed in 1834 in opposition to the "King Jackson" whom they viewed as a tyrant that abused his executive power. They were formed based on the Whig Party of Great Britain that opposed Monarchy. Just like them, the American Whig Party believed in small government and limited power. They become the GOP or Grand Old Party which was named the Anti-Slavery Republican Party in 1854. The main plank in their platform was the abolishment of slavery and they were formed to oppose the Democrat Party.[22]

The Democrats stronghold of political power was in the South where there were approximately 4 million slaves prior to 1861.[23] If these slaves were freed, the rich plantation owners would lose millions of dollars because they would have to pay workers and actually treat them like humans. Slaves were a huge part of the economy in the South and the rich, the powerful, and the politicians knew the monetary benefit of keeping slavery legal. Not only would they lose money, but if they were recognized as citizens, then their vote could turn the tide of elections and democrats would lose power and prestige. This could not be tolerated.

In order to justify slavery to keep their political power, people needed a reason other than just money. Slavery has always been a part of human existence. In fact, most of the modern world allowed slavery due to economics, poverty, dominion of a conquered people etc. Almost every nation recognized slavery as a valid part of the human condition when America was founded.

The problem was not with slavery, but with the American ideals of freedom and justice and the abhorrence of the power of the King of England ruling with an iron fist.

The Democrats had to keep the European view of black people as sub human at the forefront of American policy if they wanted slavery to thrive in this country. Keep in mind that NOT A SINGLE SLAVE OWNER WAS REPUBLICAN. Remember that the Republican Party was specifically formed to END slavery.

Several lies had to be propagated in order to keep the slave trade in a new country that was founded on the freedom of the individual. One lie was simply that blacks were not people or were less than other races. Slaves were not permitted to learn to read or write based on this narrative. Slaves could be beaten, and in fact were beaten worse than most people treat their animals. If they weren't the same as other people, then they could be treated differently.

Another lie was that slavery was actually better for blacks than freedom. It was argued that black people were incapable of caring for themselves, holding skilled jobs, contributing to society, or being decent civilized human beings in general. The fact that many slaves sang songs at night was likely used as evidence that slaves were happy with their circumstances.   These lies ignored the facts that other blacks owned slaves and that slaves frequently escaped and made lives for themselves in Northern States and in Canada.

To make a long story short, Lincoln became President, and in January 1863 he signed the Emancipation Proclamation which freed the slaves. The Democrats knew that if these newly freed individuals were given the same rights as citizens that they would vote for the people of the party that freed them. This is why Democrats vehemently fought Civil Rights every step of the way. Here are the things they voted against:

The Thirteenth Amendment (Amendment XIII) to the United States Constitution abolished slavery and involuntary servitude, except as punishment for a crime. In Congress, it was passed by the Senate on April 8, 1864, and by the House on January 31, 1865. 86 Republicans and only 14 Democrats voted yes.

The Fourteenth Amendment (Amendment XIV) to the U.S. Constitution, ratified on July 9th

1868, granted citizenship to all persons born or naturalized in the United States—including former slaves—and guaranteed all citizens "equal protection of the laws." Not a single Democrat voted to pass it.

The Fifteenth Amendment (Amendment XV) to the U.S. Constitution prohibits the federal and state governments from denying a citizen the right to vote based on that citizen's "race, color, or previous condition of servitude". It was ratified on February 3, 1870. The vote in the House was 144 to 44, with 35 not voting. Zero Democrats supported the bill and only 3 Republicans voted against it, some because they thought the amendment did not go far enough in its protections. The final vote in the Senate was 39 to 13 and all 39 votes were Republicans.

The Civil Rights Act of 1964 outlaws discrimination based on race, color, religion, sex, or national origin. It prohibits unequal application of voter registration requirements, racial segregation in schools, employment, and public accommodations. It was passed on July 2nd, 1964 with 79% of Republicans voting yes, without which, it would not have passed. 91 Democrats voted NO and 9 refused to vote.[25]

Jim Crow laws and the idea of "separate but equal" became a way of life in every Democrat controlled city and state. The rise of the KKK as the enforcement arm of the Democrat party grew in strength. During Reconstruction, many black men were elected to Southern state legislatures as Republicans, and 22 black Republicans served in the U.S. Congress by 1900. The 1924 "Klanbake" Democrat Convention Sheds Light on Democratic Party History if you care to learn more about the history of racism in politics in America.

The point is simple. There are always those who would use racism for political purposes. The facts speak for themselves. If the politicians could foster racism in our society, they could keep their power. This is why racism has played such a big part in our society and in politics in particular. It was used as a means to an end; power and money.

This is merely the example of America. Racism has played a major role in many countries politics. Currently racism is playing a huge role in South Africa among several other nations. In history, racism played a major role in Germany.

The question is, do we know the history, and do we actually learn from it to PREVENT it? I fear that some politicians have learned from it merely in order to refine it and use it as a weapon to retain power.

<u>The Big Switch</u>

There are those who would deceive you to wield the power of racism for their political gain in America today. The big lie that they are perpetuating now is that the American political parties switched places ideologically and that the Democrats of today are well intentioned, civil rights supporters, and lovers of the common people. They deny history and have no problem labelling all Republicans as evil, hateful, bigoted, racist, xenophobic, war mongers based on the made up "fact" that Republicans have always been the party of racism.

The fact is this: ONLY TWO OR THREE RACIST DIXIECRATS SWITCHED SIDES during the time of the Dixiecrats and subsequent racism in our politics. The only one that is thoroughly documented is Strom Thurmond.[26] Thurmond was a leader in the KKK and was originally a Democrat. After the Democrats failed to stop the Civil Rights Act of 1964, he resigned from the Democrat Party in protest and angrily switched to the Republican Party.

Racism Caused by Personal Experience

This reason for racism is often not as permanent as the others because people constantly have new experiences. If a person experiences bad things several times in their life, and it always happens to be by the same race of person, they can often develop a stereotype about that race. To a person of weak character, this quickly develops into racism. The only good thing about this type of racism is that it can easily be remedied by new experiences that are the opposite. As soon as someone sees that not all people of that skin color will treat him or her badly, they can begin to change their opinion.

This is similar to a dog that is beaten by a man when it is a pup. Over time, the dog begins to distrust all males. Those who do not use their brains develop the same type of reaction to experiences they have had. Weak or flawed people cannot separate their bad experiences with a few people from ALL people who happen to look like the bad people.

A logical person quickly learns that each individual is different and is in no way tied to someone they have never met. If they were, then everyone who wears a certain color shirt or shoes would all act the same, or everyone with the same color hair would all act the same. This is a ridiculous association to make, and yet; some people can never break free from their early experiences.

A smart and logical person learns from their own mistakes. A wise person learns from the mistakes of others.

<u>Racism Caused by Logic and Science</u>

"Nature is always teaching us ... that she is governed by the principle of selection: that victory is to the strong and the weak must go to the wall. She teaches us that what may seem cruel to us, because it affects us personally or because we have

been brought up in ignorance of her laws, is nevertheless often essential if a higher way of life is to be attained. Nature ... knows nothing of the notion of humanitarianism which signifies that the weak must at all costs be surrounded and preserved even at the expense of the strong... Nature does not see in weakness any extenuating reasons ... on the contrary, weakness calls for condemnation.... War is therefore the unalterable law of the whole of life — the prerequisite for the natural selection of the strong and the precedent for the elimination of the weak. What seems cruel to us is from Nature's point of view entirely obvious. A people that cannot assert itself must disappear and another must take its place. All creation is subject to this law; no one can avoid it... Since life on earth began, struggle has been the very essence of existence." – Adolf Hitler speaking before cadets on June 22, 1944 [20]

The idea of Racism can come from several sources, but at its root is the belief that one race is inferior to others or that one race is superior. This is the natural outcome of the Theory of Evolution. Darwin's idea of "the survival of the fittest" is also a natural product of the Theory of Evolution. Supposing that all life began in some primordial soup and eventually the right chemical compounds and electricity came together in just the right way to create the first single-celled organism, then the idea of mutations creating various new things is plausible. Those who believe in Evolution without the hand of a divine creator or some alternate higher power directly responsible for creating species, must believe in a progression of mutations over time that create new species. If not, there is no such thing as Evolution.

Assuming this to be true, Evolution requires a multitude of eradications or eliminations of unfit forms of species many times over until the species is perfected by multiple advanced and good mutations. These mutations supposedly occur over vast periods of times, in which the bad mutations cannot allow the species to survive and they naturally die out. The process of getting rid of these poor sub-standard mutations comes in various forms. Some scientists propose that the poorer genetic stock is easily devoured by predators, while others assume that the poorer mutations actually inhibit growth, propagation, or life itself, and the individual dies naturally. For example, a frog born with poorly developed (or mutated) lungs would have difficulty breathing and would either asphyxiate itself or be readily captured and eaten by a predator because it could not summon enough oxygen to leap out of the way.

As a species evolves from one species into another, the various in between forms or "missing links" face mass extinctions due to their unfitness. The transition from whales to land mammals, or from lizards to birds, or even apes to humanoids, or vice versa, all require thousands of years if not hundreds of thousands or even millions depending on which Evolutionist you speak to. Some say that these transitions took so long that the in-between species fossils just don't show up in the record.

Some scientists, realizing that this is highly illogical, have adopted the "punctuated equilibrium" view. This view states that massive amounts of mutations occurred to create a new species in a relatively short time period, separated by vast amounts of time in which little or no mutations occurred. This allows them to claim that there would be no in-between fossils because evolution happened too fast. Either view still readily concedes the fact that millions of mutations must occur for a new species to be perfected, and thus hundreds of millions of unfit forms must die in the process. This is simply "survival of the fittest" and is a natural selection of nature with no moral implication to it.

Obviously, a species in transition will have different traits that affect its ability to survive. Those forms lower down on the Evolutionary chain will have inferior traits and will be less likely to have a positive contribution to the gene pool. They naturally die out over time, but usually this process takes many generations. These traits may be obvious to some in the species, and they may cannibalize or ostracize the inferior form. Whether eaten by predators or pushed out of the group by those animals higher on the Evolutionary ladder, the end result is that the inferior ones die and/or are not allowed to pass on their inferior DNA and inferior mutations.

When a species is able to readily identify these poor mutations, like a limb that doesn't work properly or the runt of the litter, then they are able to more quickly eliminate that drain on the gene pool. This is how Evolutionists explain an animal eating the runt of its litter, or pushing the weaker one out of the way and not allowing it to suckle at its mother's teat. This "natural selection" or "survival of the fittest" is supposed to naturally weed out the weaker or inferior ones of the species. Taking the weak ones out of the competition for a sexual mate leaves only the normal and the better mutations. This makes it easier for those that are better equipped to survive to pass on their genes to the next generation.

If humans have indeed evolved from apes, it is safe to assume that mankind is still evolving and getting better as a species. I have never met anyone, evolutionist or theist, who believes that mankind is perfect and has reached the pinnacle of our existence. Evolution would require continued mutations and the advancement of the human race, either into a more perfect species or into some other species entirely. Evolution is the continued mutation of genes and species by chance. It cannot stop at humans because it happens by chance and there is no mechanism for stopping random mutations. There is no design in Evolution. It is merely a continuous happenstance that nobody can control. The natural selection of the better mutations can be sped up or slowed, depending on various circumstances and the ability of the inferior ones to breed or not, but natural selection will never be stopped.

This is all accepted Evolutionary Theory; nobody disputes this who believes in evolution. These facts (assuming evolution to be true) are a requirement for evolution to work. Given these facts, it stands to reason that humans are still evolving. If evolution is true and humans are evolving, then some humans MUST be more evolved than others. A true believer in evolution would see this and would begin looking for ways to help the species progress to the next level of evolutionary development. This means that those people who want to help must determine which of the species are advanced and which are inferior. The best way to help human kind achieve the advancement of our species would be to prevent the inferior ones from propagating their inferior DNA.

Evolution of the species could take several turns, either intellectual, physical, or both. Physical evolution would be the easiest to see, but intellectual evolution could be seen almost as easily if groups of people excelled as a society or somehow advanced faster than other groups. As far as physical evolution goes, the obvious thing would be to see which humans were closest to our supposed evolutionary ancestors, the apes. Dark skin, hairy bodies, high brows, large sloping foreheads, elongated muscles of the arms and legs, etc. would all point to a less evolved person who is closer in structure to apes than the new and improved evolved human.

Intellectual evolution could be seen by examining cultures that have elevated standards of living, hygiene, and technology. Less evolved cultures would be those that still live in rudimentary villages, have less evolved technologically, and are more primitive in hygiene and eating habits. Logically, those societies that live better, have a longer life span, enjoy less stress, and have a vast store of knowledge or capability to learn, will have a greater chance of breeding and a better gene pool than the former societies.

The point is simply this. A society that believes in evolution must eventually see the needs of the many to outweigh the needs of the few. This should naturally lead to extermination of the lower developed humanoids to speed the survival of the fittest. The natural conclusion if examined with a purely logical and evolutionary lens, is that certain societies (i.e.: 3rd world) are obviously less developed than others and thus they are intellectually less evolved and should be wiped out for the betterment of the species.

The second conclusion is that certain races (i.e.: physical characteristics) are less apelike than others and thus more evolved. If only the advanced races are left to propagate, then only the better mutations will survive and it will speed the evolutionary process and help future generations to achieve more and be better. Who doesn't want to help the children of the future?

It finally comes down to this. Which race is more advanced, which race is "The Master Race"? Evolution breeds racism, plain and simple. Adolf Hitler proved that. From his own book <u>Mein Kampf</u>, or <u>My Struggle</u> in English, he sets forth his arguments based on evolution.

His book is full of history to include a logical study of mankind and civilizations. His conclusions are flawed and obviously resulted in acts of the most horrific nature. Hitler's crowning moment in his eyes was the concentration camps and his almost successful attempt to exterminate an entire race of people. If you want to talk about ripping children from parents, or injustice of any kind, or torture (waterboarding etc.), or any number of modern day controversial topics; one has only to study the Holocaust and the things Hitler had doctors and soldiers do to other human beings to find out what evil really is.

Everything in his book comes down to his idea of salvation of the human race. He felt that the Evolutionary concept of "survival of the fittest" was the core governing principle of "Mother Nature". Humans had subverted it by extending welfare and creating societies where the "unfit" were allowed to survive and breed indiscriminately. Humankind's weakness of carrying for those less fortunate was polluting its gene pool and perverting nature's intent to better itself. The most important thing that a well-meaning and caring human could do was to educate the world and cleanse the world of the lower classes of humans. In this way mankind would produce the best and evolve into the best possible humans. Hitler literally felt that he was doing mankind a favor with his crimes against humanity and his acts of war.

In Mein Kampf Chapter 11 titled "Race and People" Hitler outlines this philosophy which permeates his book and his adult life:

> *"Just as Nature concentrates its greatest attention, not to the maintenance of what already exists but on the selective breeding of offspring in order to carry on the species, so in human life also it is less a matter of artificially improving the existing generation – which, owing to human characteristics, is impossible in ninety-nine cases out of a hundred – and more a matter of securing from the very start a better road for future development."* [24 pg. 24]

Hitler believed that Nature was some guiding force that should not be messed with. This "Nature" had a goal of better development of all species through natural selection. The purest form of the species needed to mate with other pure forms to create a more fit offspring. Those could then mate with others of its kind to create an even better offspring. So on and so forth until the ultimate goal of nature was reached via the guiding hand of Evolution.

To this end, he saw intermingling of human races to be a detriment to the greater plan. Hitler looked at human history through this lens and thus everything he looked at was the result of race.   In his view, all cultures had a primarily racial component and thus the fate of every culture throughout history was due to race. Either it excelled due to racial purity, or it fell as a result of racial impurity i.e.: higher evolved beings mating with lower ones and producing inferior offspring.

Hitler states:

"All the great civilizations of the past became decadent because the originally creative race died out, as a result of contamination of the blood [propagation of mixed-race children]." [24 pg. 126]

"If we divide mankind into three categories – founders of culture, bearers of culture, and destroyers of culture – the Aryan alone can be considered as representing the first category." [24 pg.127]

Hitler was obsessed with the development of HIS culture (German) and thus his race. He viewed the Aryan race and the German culture as the most civilized and his view of history showed that. In his estimation there was no such thing as a moral right or wrong, only whether or not it contributed to the betterment of the human race as a whole. In other words, if whites [a German type culture] are able to build a better city/civilization, then any treatment of lower humans [any other race than his] was acceptable. As poet laureate Alfred Tennyson once said, *"Nature is red in both tooth and claw"*.

> *"For the establishment of superior types of civilization the members of inferior races formed one of the most essential prerequisites. They alone could supply the lack of mechanical means without which no progress is possible. It is certain that the first stages of human civilization were not based so much on the use of tame animals as on the employment of human beings who were members of an inferior race.*
>
> *…*
>
> *"As a conqueror, he [the Aryan race] subjugated inferior races and turned their physical powers into organized channels under his own leadership, forcing them to follow his will and purpose. By imposing on them a useful, though hard, manner of employing their powers he not only spared*

the lives of those whom he had conquered but probably made their lives easier than these had been in the former state of so called 'freedom'. While he ruthlessly maintained his position as their master, he not only remained master but he also maintained and advanced civilization."

...

"The adulteration of the blood and racial deterioration conditioned thereby are the only causes that account for the decline of ancient civilizations"-Adolf Hitler [24 pg. 129]

This belief is not uncommon in the minds of those who profit from racism and slavery. If you do a careful study of slavery in the United States, this sentiment was often put forth by the KKK and the Democrat party. They tried to spread the idea that slavery actually raised the standard of living for a poor black person and thus was better for him and his family than freedom.

Hitler had a loftier goal. Do not forget that he saw mankind's kindness and caring for the poor and downtrodden individual as a weakness. Taking care of an invalid or mentally inferior person was thwarting nature's ability to ensure the survival of the fittest. Empathy and sympathy are both character flaws in this view. It allows the heart to get in the way of what is viewed as logical. Logically, caring about the well-being of the entire human race for all future generations is much more important than say, the continuation of a small segment of the current population. Billions and billions of future children's quality of life, freedom, and mental ability weighed against a few millions of one inferior race is the equivalent of asking if you would rather save 1000 people or just one terminally ill person who has outlived their usefulness.

I would venture to say that many people reading this do not have a problem with that scenario of a terminally ill person having their life "humanely" ended against their will to save 1000 others. If so, your core beliefs ought to be examined. Self-reflection is a noble quality that few possess, and fewer still are able to wisely make changes based on what they learn. Unfortunately for the world, Hitler had that quality of self-reflection, but his mind was twisted and we can see how that played out on the world stage. Those who don't have a problem with the above scenario and who think that the terminally ill patient should be killed to save the life of the

1000 have the same mind that Hitler did. If you can justify murdering one person, logically you could justify murdering 1,000 or 8,000,000 just like Hitler did.

It is interesting to note that the American society is drifting further down this rabbit hole which started with this exact same philosophy when it comes to Eugenics and Euthanasia. Eugenics is the idea of selective breeding of only those deemed desirable and sterilization of those deemed less desirable so that the population ends up being of a certain type of human instead of all types. The people that get to determine what is desirable are of course those who force the sterilization on others. This is almost always started out with a benign goal of healthcare and preventing unwanted or dangerous pregnancy. This is in fact how and why Margaret Sanger started the organization known as Planned Parenthood.

Margaret Sanger had significant influence in America and started several organizations along with her colleagues in the field of Eugenics. One of them, the American Betterment Foundation focused on forced sterilization of undesirables. Another one was the American

Birth Control League (ABCL) which was focused on stopping the pregnancies of undesirables. This later became known as Planned Parenthood. It is no secret that even to this day the majority of abortions performed are on black women, killing black children. Nor is it a secret that they have always concentrated their "centers" near densely populated black communities. After Sanger died in 1966 this organization tried to distance itself from its Eugenics and racist roots to present itself as a Civil Rights organization for Women's Rights. They have succeeded, however hypocritical and false their public image is.

These are a few of Margaret Sanger's associates. The old adage that "birds of a feather flock together" is certainly true in her case.

Dr. S. Adolphus Knopf was a member of her ABCL and he spoke at a March 1925 meeting for International Birth Control in New York City. He warned of the menace of the *"black"* peril to white societies.

Lothrop Stoddard, was a Harvard graduate and the author of The Rising Tide of Color against White Supremacy and he was also an associate and follower of

Sanger. Stoddard described the eugenic practices of the Third Reich as *"scientific"* and *"humanitarian."*

Dr. Harry Laughlin, another board member of the ABCL spoke of purifying America's human *"breeding stock"* and purging America's *"bad strains."* He also included shiftless and poor whites in his description of the *"Negro problem"*.

Margaret Sanger spoke of sterilizing those she designated as *"unfit,"* a plan she said would be the *"salvation of American civilization"*. She founded the Birth Control Review in 1917. Some of her articles include: "Some Moral Aspects of Eugenics" (June 1920), "The Eugenic Conscience" (February 1921), "The purpose of Eugenics" (December 1924), "Birth Control and Positive Eugenics" (July 1925), "Birth Control: The True Eugenics" (August 1928).

The following excerpt is from <u>A Plan for Peace</u> by Margaret Sanger which was published in Birth Control Review (April 1932, pp. 107-108):

d. to apply a stern and rigid policy of sterilization and segregation to that grade of population whose progeny is tainted, or whose inheritance is such that objectionable traits may be transmitted to offspring.

e. to insure the country against future burdens of maintenance for numerous offspring as may be born of feebleminded parents, by pensioning all persons with transmissible disease who voluntarily consent to sterilization.

f. to give certain dysgenic groups in our population their choice of segregation or sterilization.

g. to apportion farm lands and homesteads for these segregated persons where they would be taught to work under competent instructors for the period of their entire lives.

The first step would thus be to control the intake and output of morons, mental defectives, epileptics.

The second step would be to take an inventory of the secondary group such as illiterates, paupers, unemployables, criminals, prostitutes, dope-fiends; classify them in special departments under government medical protection, and segregate them on farms and open spaces as long as necessary for the strengthening and development of moral conduct.

Having corralled this enormous part of our population and placed it on a basis of health instead of punishment, it is safe to say that fifteen or twenty millions of our population would then be organized into soldiers of defense---defending the unborn against their own disabilities.

...

With the future citizen safeguarded from hereditary taints, with five million mental and moral degenerates segregated, with ten million women and ten million children receiving adequate care, we could then turn our attention to the basic needs for international peace.

As a strong supporter of eugenics, Sanger wrote:

"It is said that a fish as large as a man has a brain no larger than the kernel of an almond. In all fish and reptiles where there is no great brain development, there is also no conscious sexual control. The lower down in the scale of human development we go the less sexual control we find. It is said that the aboriginal Australian, the lowest known species of the human family, just a step higher than the chimpanzee in brain development, has so little sexual control that police authority alone prevents him from obtaining sexual satisfaction on the streets."-Sanger, "What Every Girl Should Know" 1920, p. 47).

In her book "Women and the New Race" Sanger advocated for a "new race" and eventually a "super race" of genetically superior people. Her associates Leon Whitney, president of the American Eugenics Society, and Madison Grant, who extolled the Nordic race and bemoaned its "corruption" both received letters from Adolph Hitler praising them and their research.

Grant wrote a book called The Passing of the Great Race in which he said,

"Mistaken regard for what are believed to be divine laws and a sentimental belief in the sanctity of human life tend to prevent both the elimination of defective infants and the sterilization of such adults as are themselves of no value to the community. The laws of nature require the obliteration of the unfit and human life is valuable only when it is of use to the community or race."

It is certainly not hard to see how Hitler found some of the justification for his ideology and practices in this new "scientific" field of Eugenics which has its basis in the theory of Evolution and the propagation of a better species.

While Eugenics is the idea of promoting positive gene pools through the elimination of poor genes at birth or prior to it, Euthanasia is the other end of the spectrum. Euthanasia is the practice of ending the life of someone deemed terminally ill, too old, unfit, unseemly, or beyond the limits of their usefulness. Both Eugenics and Euthanasia were started in America as "science" and both ended up being used by Hitler in Nazi Germany as his logical propaganda that resulted in the murder of over 8 million people in a very

short time. His propaganda went something like
this;

> We are overpopulating the planet.
> The desirables don't have enough kids and
>   the undesirables have too many.
> The overpopulation of unfit and
>   undesirables creates a lack of jobs
>   and poor conditions.
> The poor can't help themselves and
>   increase the problem with more
>   children.
> There is too much crime and war because
>   of these problems.
> The primary cause of the problems is that
>   we allow the filthy, diseased,
>   disabled, undesirables, and criminals
>   to continue to breed.
> We must identify and sterilize those
>   undesirables for the benefit of the
>   human race.

Then Hitler went on to explain how the
Aryan race was the saviors of the world and the
Jews were the denizens of society and the cause
of every malady known to man.

"The Jew offers the most striking contrast to the Aryan." [24 pg. 131]

"That is why the Jew systematically endeavors to lower the racial quality of a people by permanently adulterating the blood of the individuals who make up that people." [24 pg. 142]

"If we review all the causes which contributed to bring about the downfall of the German people we shall find that the most profound and decisive cause must be attributed to the lack of insight into the racial problem and especially in the failure to recognize the Jewish danger." [24 pg. 143]

Once he had established that Jews were the problem he was able to begin making laws to discriminate. Believe it or not, one of the main places Hitler got his ideas was from the policies and laws of the American Democrat Party. The new *"science"* of Eugenics and Euthanasia and the segregation of blacks in America were both a justification for, and a source for his propaganda and new laws.

It seems obvious to most logical people, especially if they actually learned history, that Hitler was a twisted man who attempted to justify his barbaric, genocidal, evil plan by using science and racism as his excuse. There are some who attribute it to Christianity, but this is easily refuted in his own writing where he laughed at religion and saw it as a way to dupe the masses into following him.

> *"There is something very unhealthy about Christianity," Hitler opined. "As far as we are concerned, we've succeeded in chasing the Jews from our midst and excluding Christianity from our political life. ... The heaviest blow that ever struck humanity was the coming of Christianity. Bolshevism is Christianity's illegitimate child. Both are inventions of the Jew... Christianity is an invention of sick brains: one could imagine nothing more senseless."* [27] *– Adolf Hitler*

The only way Hitler saw "Religion" or "God" influencing him was in the spiritualization of "Mother Nature" guiding him to do her bidding of eliminating lower species of man.

"At that time my lot in life seemed to me a harsh one; but to-day I see in it the wise workings of Providence. The Goddess of Fate clutched me in her hands..."[24] pg. 20
– Adolf Hitler

<u>The End Result of Racism</u>

Racism comes from either a twisted mind or an evil one. There can be no doubt that hating a person or treating them differently merely because they are a certain color is simply illogical and ultimately wrong. Racism can only lead to two outcomes. Either the racist person still adheres to some moral code of right and wrong and merely internalizes their bigotry and hatred, or they let it influence their speech and actions and actually harm others.

In the case of the one who does not let racism influence their actions, they become more hateful and twisted as time goes on. That type of character that despises other humans for no reason other than the superficial color of their skin is one that eats away at a person. Either they confront it and drastically change their world view, or it begins to pour out of them in vile speech and actions. ANY time someone judges another by the color of their skin; it is a reflection of their own poor character and evil intentions. Moral judgements can only be legitimately made based on someone's words and actions. Racists, while judging others, are simply revealing the judgement that they deserve. Their degrading words and actions prove that they themselves are rotten to the core and do not deserve the time of day.

A society that lauds a racist person and gives them a platform to speak (such as a news station anchor job, or position in politics, or management at some office) deserves to be judged. America's laws do not allow for racism. Our Constitution now forbids separate treatment of people based on color. As such, our society has chosen to end systematic and institutionalized racism.

A person who resorts to violence due to racism is quickly prosecuted like any other criminal. In America, a crime is a crime regardless of the race of the person who commits the crime, or the race of the victim. I challenge you to find a modern day (in the last 50 years) murder where a judge, police officer, or lawyer stated that it wasn't really murder because of the person's skin color. In the same manner, you cannot find a robbery and assault crime where the person was not prosecuted because of their skin color. You won't find it. You can assume, infer, or make claims that it happens, but you cannot PROVE it because if you could, that person would be prosecuted according to our laws.

Remember that you can never legislate morality in a free society. That is why we do not force people to believe in God, or force women to cover their ankles, or force people to swear to eat healthy etc. etc. People's morals change. Thoughts cannot be judged. What we can do, and what America has done, is put laws in place to protect everyone's rights regardless of skin color. A free people can never outlaw racism without having some sort of "thought police" who try to determine what people think. There will always be racist people, and that is why you should choose your friends wisely and learn to judge people's character so that you do not surround yourself with such evil.

What we CAN do, is outlaw racist treatment and crimes, regardless of the victims' skin color. This is what America has done. We are a nation of laws. We are a melting pot of every skin color and nationality. We prosecute crime without regard to the color of a persons' skin. (Whether or not someone has money and is not prosecuted to the fullest extent of the law because of that is a whole different issue that is not going to be addressed in this book).

The final answer on this issue is that racism always results in either an ugly person or an ugly crime. Racism on a national level always leads to an evil society and frequently leads to genocide as in Nazi Germany.

Chapter 4: LGBT, Muslims, and Other Discriminated Groups

This idea that it is somehow legal or okay in our society to openly discriminate against any group is completely a false claim. You cannot find a single law in present day America that allows for such bigotry. There is not a single company in America that allows such discrimination.

Find one. Then I will print a retraction.

Anyone who states that women's rights are being taken away, or gay rights are being taken away, or the President is trying to take away "insert special group here" rights, are wrong. They are simply lying or manipulating truth to tug at your heartstrings. If they can get you angry about some perceived injustice, then they have control over you and gain your support. The fact is that not a single person in America has fewer rights than another unless you count the unborn child in the argument.

Find a single right that straight, white, Christian, males have in America that anyone else does not have. You can't. Anything they can do legally, you and I can do as well.

I'll wait.

I'll print a retraction with your name honorably mentioned.

Sorry, but if you believe that it is legal, in America, to discriminate or treat any of those groups differently, you have been lied to.

Chapter 5: The New Racism in America

Unfortunately, it is becoming cool to be racist in America again. This was brought about by several means. One, we have begun teaching racism in our public institutions. Two, we have a national media that is subsidized by our federal government that promotes it. Three, we have many in our government who openly support racism and racist policies.

In my opinion, this must be met with complete and total dismantling of our public schools, media, and Congress. They must literally be de-funded, torn down, and destroyed. Every teacher, congressman, and news personality must be blackballed from ever having influence again, and the institutions rebuilt from the foundation up. It won't happen, but I believe it is the only way to fix it.

Let me explain and then let me provide proof. Please read until the end of this chapter and then judge for yourself. Open your eyes to what you see in our society and wake up to what we are teaching our children. We are reaching an age where right is called wrong, and evil (racism) is being called right. If we don't radically change this view in our society, then we are no longer civilized. It is time for the uncomfortable truth to be confronted.

American society openly advocates for racism against WHITE people.

Yes, I said it.

It's the truth.

If you think about how many times you have heard the term "old, white men" on television or the radio you will realize that people are casting dispersions on only certain men because of the color of their skin. It is a vile and racist thing to put down someone simply because they were born a certain color.

If you are prone to argue against this because "it's true", or "white people ARE the problem", or any other "but white people", then you must face the fact that **you** are racist. Learn to self-reflect and change yourself before it is too late. Don't become the ugly, twisted, evil, racist that you pretend to abhor.

"White privilege" has become a common term in our society. It denotes the false idea that the color of someone's skin automatically gives them special privileges that others do not have in America. This is blatantly false. The argument is that American society was built by white people, for white people, and that it inherently confers a special privilege upon those who are born with that skin color. This "privilege" gives white children a better education and a better chance for success in life.

Not only that, but "white privilege" carries with it an implied concept that the person who has been so unfairly advantaged must be racist because they have taken the advantages in life from those of another color skin. If a white person denies this white privilege, then they are automatically deemed wrong and ignorant at the very least. At the worst, it is deemed proof positive of their racism. This horrendous lie is completely false on multiple levels.

First, the economics of capitalism and our free society is such that there is no "pot of wealth" or privilege that exists. If one person has wealth or a certain privilege, this in no way takes away from the whole. Nobody else is hurt because one person is extremely wealthy or goes to a high quality school. There is no such thing as "distribution of wealth" or distribution of anything else in America. Nobody decides who gets stuff and who gets certain advantages in our society. Wealth is created, earned, and inherited from family; it is not scooped together into some pot and doled out at the whims of evil white people.

The only deciding factor in how much advantage you have in life is YOU. Your decisions to work hard, go to school, get married, not get into debt, etc. are only yours to make. Nobody holds a gun to your head and forces you to have unprotected sex or to use a credit card. Your desire to have an I-Phone, a new car, cable television, etc. can be controlled by you alone. If you can't afford it, get another job or stop going to movies and eating out. Save your money and pay for what you want with cash. It is amazing what some good financial discipline will bring you and how successful you can become if you have patience and save while you work hard.

Anyone can get a job at a gas station. Anyone can work three jobs while going to college and pay their own way like I did. Anyone can join the military and learn a high-tech job and even have the military pay for their college. Six years in the military with no debt is a lot better than four years in college with a $100,000 debt.

Second, privilege in America is the result of earned income and usually a lifetime of hard work. It has nothing to do with the color of skin. For example, do an internet search on the wealth or success of these people and tell me if the color of their skin earned it for them:

Allen West

Candace Owens

Oprah Winfrey

Barack Obama

Morgan Freeman

Tiger Woods

Maxine Waters

LeBron James

Beyoncé Knowles

Will Smith

Serena Williams

Eric Holder

Ta-Nehisi Coates

Mary Jackson (aerospace engineer)

Michael Jordan

Privilege for these individuals and for millions of others came because of hard work, a desire to excel, dedication, time and effort. Some people get lucky by randomly stumbling into the right person who can propel them to success; others get lucky by stumbling into the right place at the right time and striking it rich. Neither of those random circumstances has anything to do with the color of one's skin.

People may "feel" that being white in 2018 gives you some advantage in our society, but it does not. The way you carry yourself, the way you dress, the way you present yourself in terms of personal hygiene and language, and the things you do and say is what gives you advantage in America. If you walk into a bank with your pants sagging, tattoos all over your face, smelling of alcohol and smoke, and angrily demand to see the manager about a job, it doesn't matter what color your skin is, you have about a 100% chance of not getting the job and maybe even getting the cops called on you. However; if you take a shower, don't have face tattoos, cut your hair, wear a pressed suit that is clean, and respectfully in clear English ask to fill out a job application and speak to the manager, you have a good chance of getting an interview and possibly the job... no matter what your race is.

To those who would argue that speaking English correctly, dressing neatly, and wearing a belt are "White Culture" and it is racism to demand others to conform, I call B.S. Those people are in fact the racists. They think that minorities are too stupid to know how to use a belt and tuck in their shirts? They think that minorities are too ignorant to speak proper

English politely and in a respectful tone of voice? The sagging pants, in your face attitude, and poor English culture is gang culture NOT racial culture. Uneducated and rebellious people of all races do those things. Claiming that a respectful, clean, and neat person who knows how to dress properly is conforming to white culture is actually a racist statement.

White privilege is a myth used to perpetuate two ideas. The first is that white people are somehow not deserving of what they have and didn't have to work as hard for it as other races. The second is that white people are inherently racist (which is a bad character quality). Assuming that someone has bad character simply because of the pigmentation of their skin is a racist assumption.

Both ideas perpetuated by the term "white privilege" are racist and disgusting. Both ideas teach that the color of one's skin automatically determines things about them regardless of their character or actions. Both ideas are completely and utterly false and evil. ANYTIME someone makes assumptions about someone's character or worth simply based on the color of their skin, it proves that the accuser is racist.

When one is assumed to have something merely based on the color of their skin, without ever finding out that person's circumstances or character, then that assumption is racist. That is the very definition of racism and it is being taught in our society without apology. Any person accusing another of White Privilege or Black Privilege or any other privilege merely based on the color of their skin is an ignorant racist. Until you have walked in their shoes, known their life story, or understood their struggles, you have no business assuming things about them.

Here are the facts. My opinion and your opinion don't matter. Our "perspective" of the facts doesn't change the facts. Keep in mind that everyone is entitled to their opinion. Just know that some opinions are factually wrong. Remember that this chapter was started with the premise that racism has become systemic to the Media, Public Schools, and our Government.

As you read these examples, if you don't think they are racist, simply insert "Black" for the word "White". The fact that I have to advise this goes to show that you are already persuaded to think that it is okay to be hateful to white people, but not black or brown or any other color of person. Our society is already racist against whites or I would never have had to explain that.

<u>Systematic Racism in Schools</u>

I won't list too many examples, even the fascist Google (They have openly admitted to hiding certain facts and often showing web results that only share their worldview) can't hide how much White Racism is being taught in our public schools and colleges. Suffice it to say that there are literally thousands upon thousands of results when you search the web for personal experiences, news articles, and specific school problems.

Here are several articles from well-established national news sources citing proof of schools teaching white children that they are evil.

"Elite K-8 School Teaches White Students they are Born Racist" – New York Post 2016/07/01

– This teaches children that because of the color of their skin, they are evil.

"'To be white is to be racist, period,' a high school teacher told his class" – Washington Post 2016/10/19

– This Washington Post article attempts to justify this teacher's statement and make it seem like he was right.

"College professors can teach you to hate America" – Washington Post

- The University of Southern California professor Darry Sragow preaches hate to his students in his Regulation of Elections and Political Finance class, recently telling them that *"Republicans are stupid, racist losers"* and that they are *"angry old white people"*.[29]

Here are more examples of the type of education everyday Americans are being indoctrinated with:

Johnetta Benton - Hampton Middle School near Atlanta

She was recorded telling her sixth-grade students, *"America has never been*

146

great for minorities." In a tirade, she told her class: *"Because Europeans came from Europe ... you are an immigrant. You are an illegal immigrant because you came and just took it. ... You are an immigrant. This is not your country."* [28]

-Ignoring facts about history and denigrating white children simply because they are white is blatant racism and indoctrination, not to mention teaching citizens to hate their own country.

Christine Fair – Georgetown University

"Look at thus [sic] chorus of entitled white men justifying a serial rapist's arrogated entitlement. All of them deserve miserable deaths while feminists laugh as they take their last gasps. Bonus: we castrate their corpses and feed them to swine? Yes." Twitter @CChristineFair on 29 Sep 2018 at 12:54 p.m.

- This was in defense of Christine Ford, who has since been proven to have lied under oath to prevent a SCOTUS nomination by President Trump

Kevin Allred - Rutgers University in Newark, New Jersey

"Until the entire system changes – THERE ARE NO GOOD #__WHITEPEOPLE__. THERE ARE ONLY LESS BAD WHITE PEOPLE!!!" – <u>https://twitter.com/KevinAllred</u>

Noel Ignatiev - a tenured professor at Massachusetts College

"If you are a white male, you don't deserve to live. You are a cancer, you're a disease, white males have never contributed anything positive to the world! They only murder, exploit and oppress non-whites! At least a white woman can have sex with a black man and make a brown baby but what can a white male do? He's good for nothing. Slavery, genocides against aboriginal peoples and massive land confiscation, the inquisition, the holocaust, white males are all to blame! You maintain your white male privilege only by oppressing, discriminating against and enslaving others!" [31]

I could fill this book with examples. You should know that this is a common theme among almost every major university, high school, and middle school in America. Here is an excerpt from a blog post that one activist by the name of Emily Goldstein has written:

> *"I'm extremely glad that the white race is dying, and you should be too. White people do not have a right to exist. Period. That may sound like a bold statement, but it's entirely true. Any white person with even the faintest knowledge of history should curse themselves every single day for being white."* [30]

Systematic Racism in the Media

The national news media encourages this type of racist dialog on a daily basis. Almost every television station can be heard at almost all hours of the day making some statement about *"white America", "white privilege", "old white men", "the white vote", "white supremacy"* etc. It sickens me, and I don't even watch T.V. that often. Here are several examples from key T.V. personalities and major news outlets.

<u>Yes, white 'privilege' is still the problem</u> – Chicago Tribune 2018 [32]

> *"But the perception many white people have about other white people — whether it is conscious or subconscious — is that they are smarter, more ambitious, more dependable and harder working than African-Americans."*
> – This falsely labels whites as inherently racist based on a premise about how white people think. The statement itself shows that the writer is racist against white.

Don Lemon CNN October 29, 2018

> *"We have to stop demonizing people and realize that the biggest terror threat in this country is white men, most of them radicalized to the right, and we have to start doing something about them."*
> - This is blatantly hypocritical in that he says we need to stop demonizing people WHILE HE DEMONIZES WHITE MEN! Don Lemon is clearly a racist and his bigotry should never be allowed on a

national platform such as a news organization.

<u>Does White Privilege Exist in America?</u> – ABC News

> *"None of you would change places with me and I'm rich! That's how good it is to be white!" – Chris Rock[34]*

- This was during a comedy routine, but it highlights the emphasis placed on white privilege and how common it is to hear famous people express the idea. Also, the article never refutes Chris Rock's statement.

<u>White Women Who Vote GOP Aren't 'Voting Against Their Own Interests'</u> - Huffington Post 2018 [33]

> *"White women have always been ardent proponents of violent white supremacy, and they continue to be some of its most vocal advocates."*

-This is stating two lies in one, that violent white supremacy in America is a common problem among white women and that the Republican Party is a white supremacist party (never mind the fact that they were formed to fight against the white supremacy of the Democrat party).

<u>White people are still raised to be racially illiterate. If we don't recognize the system, our inaction will uphold it</u> – NBC news

> *"...as a white person, my race has meaning and grants unearned advantage... I have absorbed racist messages which may cause me to behave in racist ways- consciously or not"* – Robin DiAngelo[35]

<u>OpEd: Dear White People, Time to Use Your Privilege, Whether You Believe You Have It or Not</u> – NBC News Sept.24, 2017 [36]

Again, the list is a mile long. It is sickening how this racist idea of *"White Privilege"* is treated as newsworthy in a positive light. The media just runs rampant with their legitimization of putting down people merely based on the color of their skin. They spend hours upon hours with panels of fake "experts" dissecting the supposed "facts" that white people are inherently evil, while trying to lay a disclaimer that some whites are good and just don't realize they have this "privilege". That statement itself is racist in that it assumes that white people are too uneducated to help themselves and must have it explained to them that they are evil.

Imagine the same scenario against other races and see how you feel:

Try telling a black person that they have "Black Privilege" and are inherently evil. You see, black people in America originated in Africa, where their forefathers fought, killed, and enslaved other tribes. They then sold each other to Europeans knowing they would be beaten and killed. Black people ought to be ashamed of that heritage and the evils that their forefathers committed. The Moors in Europe did the same. Several black nations today still do the same. This is a black problem and if black Americans don't see the privilege they have in America that they did not earn, then they are obviously ignorant. – How does that sound? Do you still feel the same about saying those things to white people? Do you still feel it is okay to tell white people that they should feel ashamed of what their forefathers did and must pay for it today?

Try telling an Asian person that they have "Asian Privilege" and are inherently evil. You see, the Asian culture, whether it is Chinese, Japanese, Vietnamese, Korean, or many other nationalities, has a history of oppression and warmongering. Everyone knows of Genghis Khan, and the communism of N. Korea and Vietnam which resulted in the indiscriminate slaughter of millions. The Japanese historical culture is replete with oppression of women and training suicide soldiers called Kamikaze. Everywhere you look in Asian culture it is death and destruction and slavery. Asians in America have a higher per capita income than any other group. Asians have privilege and ought to be ashamed of the things their forefathers have done and should realize that their skin color and culture has done horrible things. If they don't realize that, then they are ignorant. – How does that sound? Still feel the same about saying those things to white people?

Try it with Hispanic people of Central and South American descent. Brown people have Brown Privilege in America and are inherently evil because of their ancestry. Their historical culture of oppression stems all the way back to the Aztec and Mayan cultures which sacrificed babies and ripped out the hearts of living victims. They destroyed entire tribes of people. Many of their countries have horrible drug cartels that wreak havoc on society and innocent families even to this day. Brown people in America have such privilege with their scholarships to colleges and affirmative action/special treatment that they are given here in America. They instead ought to be ashamed of the things their forefathers have done and should realize that their skin color and culture has done horrible things. If they don't realize that, then they are ignorant. – How does that sound? Still feel the same about saying those things to white people?

To the national news media and the pompous elite professors who dare to say these things against whites, we ought to demand their firing. Americans will not be subjugated. No child should grow up to think they are too stupid to understand things that people of other skin colors can grasp. Race DOES NOT DETERMINE one's quality of life, one's character, or one's intellect.

Systematic Racism in Government

There is a more evil racism in politics, in that it is more subtle. Politicians have to be careful about appearing bad. Many times they will twist something bad to make it appear in a good light. The way they most often cover their racism is by putting it in terms that make them appear anti-racist. Read these quotes and try to read between the lines.

Most of these quotes are from speeches where the speaker was attempting to show that they are against racism. The sad thing is that the historical context does not fit with the context of what they are speaking about. When looked at logically, many of these politicians are saying that white people today are evil, don't realize they are evil, and should be giving some of their money (taxes) to people of other races.

Put in context, stealing money via taxes from people because their forefathers might have done something wrong, these attacks against whites are completely racist.

Again, labeling a group in society as somehow evil because of their skin color is in fact a racist thing to do. Moreover; doing that while pretending to be fighting against the racism of the past is completely hypocritical and disgusting. Here are a few quotes to consider.

Maxine Waters[37]

> *"There's a history of enslaved African-Americans having to make their slave masters comfortable. This business of what we call skinning and grinning – that is something African-Americans are very much cognizant of."*

> *"This nation has always struggled with how it was going to deal with poor people and people of color"*

> *"Policy, for the most part, has been made by white people in America, not by people of color"*

> -Never mind that many blacks had been elected and put in power by Republicans before a single Democrat black person was voted into office. Never

mind that our Constitution refutes her as do all our laws today. Never mind her attempts to divide Americans based on color. Never mind that she herself is a Congresswoman whose position clearly shows the opposite of her statements.

"I'm a strong black woman, and I cannot be intimidated. I cannot be undermined."
-She is emphasizing race again, as if that is the only reason people oppose what she does.

"Most African-Americans really do believe that we are voting for our better interest in voting for Democrats"
-Again ignoring facts and again emphasizing the need to separate races or judge everything based on the color of someone's skin

Attorney General Eric Holder[38]

"I am attorney general of the United States, but I am also a black man.
-There is nothing inherently wrong with this statement, but imagine how you would feel if President Trump said it about

himself, "I am the President, but I am also a white man". Taken in light of the following additional statements, it clearly shows that this man has an animosity towards white people.

"Though this nation has proudly thought of itself as an ethnic melting pot, in things racial we have always been and I believe continue to be, in too many ways, essentially a nation of cowards"
    -Again, he emphasizes that false idea that America is racist, and I believe based on his racial bias and other statements, that he does not include himself or people of color in this idea. He clearly thinks that WHITE America is racist, and white people are cowards.

"There's a certain level of vehemence… directed at me… you know, people talking about taking their country back. There's a certain racial component to this…"
    -Clearly he believes that anyone who opposed him or the president did so out of racism against black people

"...can't imagine a time which the need for more diversity would ever cease. Affirmative action has been an issue since segregation practices. The question is not when does it end, but when does it begin...When do people of color truly get the benefits to which they are entitled?"

There it is. That is the most racist statement against ALL colors of people. This is the progressive mentality. Let's break it down:

1. White people are withholding things from people of color that they deserve.
2. This makes white people racist.
3. Black people and other minorities are being held down by whites.
4. The reason they don't succeed in life is because whites haven't given them these "things".
5. Black people NEED white people to give them things in order to succeed.
6. Minorities are too weak, ignorant, or less able than white people and that is why they need affirmative action to put them on an equal playing field with whites.

This and most other affirmative action type comments by liberals and progressives demonstrate two things. The first is their belief that minorities and blacks need something extra to be as good as white people, and they cannot succeed on their own without government help. (Which if you remember the Democrat idea that the government is mostly old white men then they are saying that minorities need the help of old white men.) The second thing is the extent to which they are willing to lie to keep people voting for them and giving them power and money as politicians.

These comments are blatant lies that they use to try to maintain their stranglehold on people's votes and thus give themselves more power. I believe that this is the secret to power on the left. They have always used minorities and blacks for their votes. Those in power continue these lies to push for more government regulation and control so that they can continue to get votes from minorities and stay in power and make money. Most politicians making such statements are vastly wealthier than the people they say they are trying to help.

The sad thing is that these policies and affirmative action type statements only serve to push the ideas that whites are racist in order to create more racist policies. Take simply the push to call voter ID laws racist. Somehow minorities are too stupid to get a government ID? Since when? Apparently those politicians believe that only white people who vote Republican are able to get a photo ID. Never mind the fact that most people in America get picture ID's since about middle school age regardless of their race. Never mind the fact that you already need a government issued picture ID to purchase alcohol, buy a gun, drive a car, go to the gym, shop at Costco, etc.

I digress. Let's continue with more racist quotes by people in government:

Attorney General Eric Holder[38]

> *"When you compare what people endured in the South in the '60s... to what happened in Philadelphia...I think does a great disservice to people who put their lives on the line for my people."* -Washington Times
> -This was in response to a question about why he did not do something as Attorney General about the Black Panthers bringing

baseball bats and batons to the polls in Philadelphia. They physically threatened people and tried to force people to vote for Barack Obama. Apparently the A.G. felt that because he was black, he should allow blacks to intimidate white voters. [39]

Cory Booker

"May the unity and spirit of the march continue to live on"
-Tweeted October 2016 with a picture of Louis Farrakhan and his million man march indicating his support for the message of the nation of Islam and its leader

"When I do my hiring in the United States Senate, I look at issues of diversity" [40]
-Proof that he sees skin color above the quality or character of his employees.

Louis Farrakhan[42]- Only listed here because apparently many politicians revere and support him. Just search for images of Farrakhan and politicians. Holder, Obama, Ellis, Waters, and many other famous politicians support his movement and invite him to political events.

Barack Obama[43]

July 24, 2009 Obama accused a white police officer of acting *"stupidly"* for arresting a black Harvard professor who accused the officer of racial profiling. It turned out that it was a justified arrest, as evidenced by police cam footage.

"You know, when Trayvon Martin was first shot, I said that this could have been my son."

-Later it was proven that Martin (a black man) had no reason to be in the neighborhood that had set up a neighborhood watch due to break-ins. When confronted he ran, and after escaping had returned to violently attack George Zimmerman with the intention to kill him by viciously slamming his head into the concrete multiple times. Zimmerman pulled his gun and shot Martin, killing him in justified self-defense.

August 14, 2014 after a white police officer was acquitted on all charges for killing Michael Brown, a black man, there were riots. It turned out that the criminal Brown had been stopped for walking down the street after a violent burglary and he attacked the police officer who stopped him. There were powder burns on his fingers and multiple eye witnesses (black individuals) who confirm that he was assaulting the officer and attempting to steal the officer's gun. This is when

Obama stated, *"We need to recognize that this is not just an issue for Ferguson, this is an issue for America"* as if it was an injustice to allow the white police officer to defend himself against a black man.

July 7, 2016 -after several other black criminals were killed (never mind that some of them were shot by fellow black men/police officers) – Obama stated, *"These are not isolated incidents. They are symptomatic of a broader set of racial disparities that exist in our criminal justice system..."* Obama was trying to push the idea that white police officers are systematically racist in America. He succeeded. A rash of police officer murders began to happen.

July 12, 2016 after five Dallas police officers were ambushed and killed during a Black Lives Matter rally, Obama didn't side with the police officers. Instead he called on police to *"acknowledge institutional racial bias"*. The so called racial bias does not exist. Police are asked to patrol places where violence and crimes happen, which in large cities happens to be most often in the ghettos and barrios where minorities live. They respond to 911 calls where the violence is and arrest those responsible.

Elijah Cummings[44]

"Many of these Americans who now are struggling to survive are Americans of color. We cannot allow it to be said by history that the difference between those who lived and those who died in the great storm and flood of 2005 was nothing more than poverty, age or skin color."
-As if somehow the storm waters sought out black people and not whites

Frederica Wilson[45]

"'The White House itself is full of white supremacists," she told the New York Times'
-after being told she was an empty barrel making noise by the White House Chief of Staff

Hakeem Jeffries[46]

"Every racist in America voted for Trump"

"Many of us are wondering why so many people who worship at the altar of white supremacy [are] drawn to Donald Trump's campaign?"

-This racist lie charges that MANY of the President's supporters are white supremacists. Using a baseless lie, spread by the media, echoed by congressmen, and the proliferation of it used as proof that it is true, is a Nazi tactic. Charging that someone is a racist or a supremacist simply because they voted for a white person is a heinous, racist, and evil thing to say.

There are literally thousands of examples in the media about white patriarchy, old white men, white America, white privilege etc. It is disgusting. Let us not even delve into the crimes committed against whites simply because of the color of their skin. This also is covered up by the media. People don't seem to get exposure to things like the disabled boy that was tortured in Chicago for being white. It was live streamed by four black men in January 2017 [47]. It was barely covered and the national news media never had panels against racism or spoke about it as a racist act.

Our government openly funds racist and segregationist policies of affirmative action and reparation. We have a Black Caucus in the government that is only made up of black representatives who openly express disdain when the President mentions that black unemployment was at its lowest point ever in U.S. History. Every time a racial quota is required or enforced, it denigrates the capabilities of the people it pretends to help. Affirmative action implicitly states that certain races would not be able to do things on their own merits without the help of the majority race. Affirmative action laws and quotas actually hurt whites that are qualified by putting someone else above them, simply based on skin color. This is overt racism under the guise of fighting racism.

White people are constantly victimized by criminals, talked about in public as being evil, denigrated in colleges and public schools, victimized by our own government via affirmative action, and publicly ridiculed and demeaned by our entire society simply based on the color of their skin. This has to stop. There is no such thing as "reverse racism". There is only racism. Racism against any color is wrong and evil.

What makes this new racism so dangerous in America is that it is not called racism. Rather, it is treated as an act against racism. It is praised, encouraged, and lifted up. Pushing to recognize and destroy so called "White Privilege", to destroy American heritage, to erase American history; all while pretending to abhor racism, is a new kind of evil that revels in hypocrisy.

One has only to do a cursory search of hate crimes, to find that most of them have been committed by the very people that they purport to be against. For instance, spray painting a black church or Jewish church with a racial message that was actually done by a member of said church. Some college campuses have had racist fliers posted across the campus that turn out to have been posted by the very people who the fliers are against. Recently a Muslim woman claimed to have been attacked by three white men who tried to pull off her hijab. She filed a hate crime, and it turns out that she lied and is being charged with a false report. [55]

This rash of crimes against minorities being committed by minorities is being done for one purpose. They want to paint white people as evil and inherently racist. The opposite is in fact true. The majority of hate crimes are being committed by minorities who are disguising their crimes as if whites have committed them. This is racist.

<u>The Myth of "White Privilege"</u>

People need to realize that there is no such thing as white privilege. Take the Great Depression for example. There was a boy by the name of Gerard Stephany that was white and grew up during this time in a large family.[48] His experience was being served breakfast by his parents in the morning and then being told to go away and not come home until night. His breakfast was usually saltine crackers and milk, and sometimes if they couldn't afford milk, only water.

This "White Privileged" boy and his siblings would go outside the city and scour the hills for berry bushes for their meals. He was too proud to beg and had the character to realize that he should work for his food and not expect a handout. Since he was too young to get a job, he would go to the parks and pick up discarded newspapers. Gerard learned to make origami roses out of the papers. He would then go to the business district at lunch time and stand at the doors of businesses and sell them for a penny. As he tells it, many people ignored him as a scrawny and dirty beggar. Some people complimented him on his industry and had enough pity on his condition to buy his flowers. Once he had earned enough, he would go and buy food to share with his brothers and sisters.

Privilege was never something he or millions of other American boys and girls had. No, they had to work, and often in harsh conditions, just to survive. At the age of seventeen in the middle of 1941, unable to find work, Gerard joined the United States Navy. He lied about his age to get in because it was the only way he could be guaranteed three meals a day. After basic training, he was put on a train to head to his first duty station when the news came out about the bombing of Pearl Harbor. The train full of new sailors was diverted, and they were ordered to go immediately to Hawaii.

His first duty was to clean up the devastation and rebuild the base at Pearl Harbor.

Later, Gerard was sent to Germany, and then the Philippines. This young boy was part of the Greatest Generation and he jumped behind enemy lines to fight the Nazi's. He fought Hitler and his armies, learned navigation by the stars, became an officer, flew dirigibles at night to spy on the enemy, and finally finished his service and retired after over 20 years of service.

I am privileged for having known this particular white boy who had the courage to stand up against real racism, the Nazis. Even though he only joined the military for three square meals a day, he did his duty bravely. It is because of millions of people like Gerard Stephany that Hitler was defeated. It is because people like him, who had no privilege, were willing to risk their life to save the world from tyranny, that America and the vast majority of the world is free today.

America is replete with stories of heroism like this by young men and women of all races. His story is not unique, and yet it is. Every person in America has a unique story to tell. Every race in America has done their part. To dehumanize, to discredit, or to reject the part that white people have played in the history of America's greatness is to be evil and racist, just as it is to do the same to any other race. To assume that someone got something because of the color of their skin and did not really earn it is to be racist.

There is no such thing as White Privilege. It is a racist term, made up by racists, and used by racists, to try and put down white people in America. They use it because they cannot effectively argue against ideas. They use it when they want to feel good about themselves. They use it as a tool to punish or discredit people that they are speaking with so that they do not have to listen to any words that person has to say. They use it to persuade minorities to agree with them and give them power so that they can rule over "We the People".

One would think that America had learned from its past, but unfortunately, it appears that we have not. Racism against white people is in vogue now as if somehow it is 'their turn' and that makes it okay. It saddens me, and should sadden you as well. We ought not to be hypocritical by allowing the racism of the past, to turn us into racists today.

174

Nobody is responsible for the sins of their fathers. Nobody should be judged based on the color of their skin. I challenge you to abhor racism. This evil should not be tolerated just because everyone expects you to. It is not okay to despise any race. It is not okay to despise white people. It is not okay to cry, "White privilege" because you had a hard time. It is never okay to think ill of someone because of what you think their forefathers might have done.

There is a big difference between a society that is racist and individuals that treat you differently because they are racist. American society as a whole has outlawed racism and despises those who are racist. Our institutions have publicly and legally denounced racism. American society is now free from institutionalized racism against minorities.

This is not to say that people do not experience racism on a personal level. There will always be those who treat others in an evil manner. We cannot deny that certain people still harbor racism in their hearts. You may encounter that on an individual level. Obviously, as I have recounted earlier in this book, I myself have experienced racism by my employer, by my schoolmates, and even saw it in the military.

A personal attack by a person because you do not have white skin, is not "White Privilege", it is personal racism. In many parts of America, in many cities, and in many jobs, having white skin is a detriment, not a privilege. What we must understand is that culture and community create these problems NOT the color of one's skin.

I will never deny that a non-White person has and probably will continue to experience discrimination in America. The fact that some White people are racist, does not say anything about the White race. It says something about that individual, that they are racist.

America is a melting pot. That means that our society as a whole allows ALL skin colors equal opportunity. Depending on your location and community and monetary privilege, you may experience discrimination no matter what your skin color is… even white. However; this does not make our society privileged for just one skin color. When you find yourself in a situation where you would be better off if your skin was a different color, you have the option and freedom to go somewhere else, or hire a lawyer.

That in itself proves the myth of white privilege. If it was true all across America and not just in your situation or your community, then you would have no hope of recourse in our justice system. Hiring a lawyer would have no chance of succeeding. Removing yourself from the situation would only put you in another similar situation. There would be no hope for people who were not white skinned.

The facts are actually the opposite of what we hear in America. We constantly hear that only whites have power, and prestige, and privilege, and opportunity in America (Obama's life dispels that falsehood). Here is the truth.

There are no "Whites only" institutions anymore. There is however a "Black Caucus" in Congress. There are Black only scholarships. There are Hispanic only scholarships. There are American Indian only scholarships. There are requirements to hire non-white people at almost every job sector in America.

If any White person started a "Whites only" anything, they would be immediately attacked for being racist, however; no one attacks anyone for making scholarships for only minority skin colors. Nobody views any minority only organization as being racist against Whites because they claim that society already has a White this, or a White that.

The reality is that America does not have any Whites only organizations. The fact that America is made up of mostly white people means that logically most organizations and institutions will be mostly white people. For example, you can argue that BET is not racist because Whites dominate every other television channel. That is false. BET specifically excludes other races. Every other channel out there does not. The fact that they are mostly White has nothing to do with racism and everything to do with the number of applicants who are White.

You could argue (and I have specifically heard this argument) that country music is only White and therefore racist and that is why you need a Black Music Awards or some other minority only style of music. This is also false. Just because certain races generally do not like a style of music does not mean that that style of music is racist. That is a logical fallacy. Country music does not exclude ANY race. If you don't like all the superstars of country music being White, then YOU should become a country music star. No one in America will stop you.

Logic is sadly lacking in our society. False equivalencies are when someone equates something to something else that it actually is NOT equal to. The above argument that a black music channel is needed because country music is all white is a false equivalence. Country music has nothing to do with the color of anyone's skin. Country music is a style. Forming a black music channel (or any color) has nothing to do with style and instead is primarily based on the color of skin. This is a false equivalency and this is racist.

If a white person and a non-white person of equal skills apply for a job in most areas of America, the non-white person gets priority. The reason is because we have laws called affirmative action that require jobs and colleges to hire and admit a certain number of minorities. This is racist.

If there is a crime committed against a minority by a White person, that victim automatically receives special attention and the term "hate crime" is frequently used. If the opposite happens, a minority commits a crime against a White person; you hear nothing about the skin color or a hate crime.

There is no "White Caucus", "White Scholarships", "White Quotas for hiring", "White Entertainment Television", "White Music Awards", "White Reel Awards", or "National Association for the Advancement of White People". It is not allowed. Where is the equality? Where is diversity when only one race is excluded from things that every other race is encouraged to do?

No. Our society has not eradicated racism. We have merely reversed it and started being racist against White people. White people are the ones not allowed to say certain phrases. White people are the ones not allowed to have organizations just for themselves. White people are the ones not allowed to have pride in their race. White people are the only ones that it has become acceptable to openly discriminate against in hiring.

180

In early 2018 Kendrick Lamar (a black singer) invited a white fan named Delaney on stage to sing one of his songs titled "M.A.A.D City" with him. The song had the word nigger in it. She sang it. He knew it was in there because he wrote the song. He invited her up on stage to sing it. When she did, he rebuked her and the crowd booed her. He made her apologize for singing the word that he wrote and invited her on stage to sing. That was deliberate racism.[56] The 'ignorant White girl' was put in her place and condemned all over the media for saying it because she should have known better.

The above referenced ABC news article even condemns her for daring to speak a word that people of her skin color should know is not allowed. That is racism. Telling people that certain skin colors can't say certain things, when others can, is discrimination based on race. Inviting them to sing a song with that word in it, just so that you can publicly condemn them is also racist. Doing that in the name of being against racism is hypocritical, deceitful, and evil to the core. Claiming to be good (against racism) while deliberately being evil (racist) and tricking an innocent person into the situation is vile.

Let's reverse the White Privilege scenario. Pretend for a moment that you are White. Pretend that you go somewhere that appears to be all one race, say a restaurant that appears to have only brown skinned people from Mexico in it. Pretend that they discriminate against you in an obvious way. Let's assume that if you were a brown skinned Mexican that they definitely would not have treated you that way. Does that mean that America has Mexican privilege? Does that mean it is always easier for Mexicans? No. It merely means that those people were racist and in that particular circumstance, you would have been better off to not be White. This is the lie of White Privilege.

Some people may say that racism against non-Whites is institutionalized in America. The big argument is that our judicial system gives unfair advantage or privilege to White people and gives harsher sentences to those of other skin colors. Individual instances should be examined identically with criminal history, circumstances, color and economic status of the jury, color of the judge, locality, etc. not just race of the criminal. Our laws are colorblind, but the judge or jury could actually be racist. If it could be proven, our laws would require a new trial and would probably disbar or jail the judge. Institutionalized racism is not real, it is illegal. Racist individuals still get hired, but if caught, they will lose that job. "White Privilege" is not institutionalized, it is illegal. It is not our society that is racist. It is individuals who are racist and who are rightfully condemned for being so.

Do people of different colors still experience "White Privilege" on occasion? I submit that the answer is emphatically NO. We still experience **RACISM** from individuals, especially in certain communities. We DO NOT experience so called "White Privilege". America has removed that and reversed it. It is no longer a privilege or a benefit nationwide to be white. It is now a detriment. In most cases across America, if a white person is up against a minority for anything, they usually lose points for being white in the eyes of our society.

Individually, you may experience what you have been conditioned to believe is "White Privilege". **In reality, what you have experienced is an evil person showing their racism.** Rise above it. Do not perpetuate it by labelling all whites with that term. It is a racist term and it merely perpetuates the racism by drawing you into it.

Stop racism. Be colorblind.

Chapter 6: How to Not Be a Racist

For those who have found that some points in this book hit too close to home, here is a simple explanation of how to detect racism and how to prevent it.

Detecting Racism

If at any time you find yourself or someone else mentioning the color of someone's skin and it is anything other than a description of what they look like, stop and think. Is the use of skin color meant to explain their character or actions? Is the use of skin color meant to incite either favor or disfavor of that person? If so, then it is racist.

If at any time you find yourself explaining away yours or someone else's success or failure by noting the color of someone's skin, then it is racism. If the conversation goes something like the following, then it is merely the description of racism which is something else entirely.

Me: I applied for a job today and the interviewer said they already had enough minorities so they weren't going to hire me.

Friend: Man, I'm sorry to hear that. They were white weren't they?

Me: Yeah, the interviewer was white and I could tell they didn't even look at my resume.

This is obviously a discussion of two people talking about a racist act, not being racist themselves. The above scenario is also completely illegal and you should retain legal counsel and sue the company should it happen to you.

If, however; you find yourself in a situation where you are not selected for a job and you have no idea why, and yet you bring up the race of the interviewer, you are being racist. No one is responsible for your success except for you. Most people get rejected for jobs many times until they are finally hired. If you retain your wits about you, you can ask the interviewer in a professional manner why they have not chosen you. Sometimes, they will tell you and you can improve yourself for the next opportunity.

How to Prevent Racism

There are a few simple things to do and to practice to stop being a racist person. Remember that most habits take repetition and a period of time to form. It is difficult to change your worldview in a day. If you are intelligent enough to recognize your racism, then you are intelligent enough to begin changing. Here are a few simple things to practice doing on a daily basis.

DON'T ever judge someone's character based on skin color.

DON'T use skin color as an excuse for failure or reason for success.

DON'T attack someone because of their skin color.

DON'T accuse someone of being racist unless you have proof they did or said something specifically with regard to race.

DO have a logical argument for your beliefs or politics, don't use race – EVER.

DO use skin color as a trait like height, weight, gender, etc. when specifically describing someone to another person,

DO call out racism when you hear friends saying or doing those things.

Preventing racism is easy, but you have to recognize it, call it out, and specifically try to stop it when you see it. Try not to be that bystander that sees evil happening and doesn't jump in to the defense of the victim.

It has been said that,

"The only thing necessary for the triumph of evil is for good men to do nothing."

Chapter 7: How Not to be a Nazi

How to recognize a Nazi

In order to not be something, you first have to know what it is. Nazi stands for Nationalsozialistische Deutsche Arbeiterpartei, or in English, National Socialist German Workers' Party. It combines two elements of politics; a strict Nationalism based on racism, and a strict socialism.

The Nationalism part was strictly German to the exclusion of all else. They went so far as to exclude rights and strip citizenship from those who were not fully German. The Socialism that was embraced was full government control of industry and the individual, with literal jack booted thugs to violently enforce it.

The 25 point platform of the Nazi party was this:

1. *We demand the union of all Germans in a Great Germany on the basis of the*

principle of self-determination of all peoples.

2. *We demand that the German people have rights equal to those of other nations; and that the Peace Treaties of Versailles and St. Germain shall be abrogated.*

3. *We demand land and territory (colonies) for the maintenance of our people and the settlement of our surplus population.* **[Free housing]**

4. *Only those who are our fellow countrymen can become citizens. Only those who have German blood, regardless of creed, can be our countrymen. Hence no Jew can be a countryman.*

5. *Those who are not citizens must live in Germany as foreigners and must be subject to the law of aliens.*

6. *The right to choose the government and determine the laws of the State shall belong*

190

*only to citizens. We therefore demand that
no public office, of whatever nature,
whether in the central government, the
province, or the municipality, shall be held
by anyone who is not a citizen.*

*We wage war against the corrupt
parliamentary administration whereby men
are appointed to posts by favor of the party
without regard to character and fitness.*

7. *We demand that the State shall above all
undertake to ensure that every citizen shall
have the possibility of living decently and
earning a livelihood. If it should not be
possible to feed the whole population, then
aliens (non-citizens) must be expelled from
the Reich.***[Living Wage]**

8. *Any further immigration of non-Germans
must be prevented. We demand that all
non-Germans who have entered Germany
since August 2, 1914, shall be compelled to
leave the Reich immediately.*

9. *All citizens must possess equal rights and duties.*

10. *The first duty of every citizen must be to work mentally or physically. No individual shall do any work that offends against the interest of the community to the benefit of all.* **[Not allowed to offend]**

   Therefore we demand:

11. *That all unearned income, and all income that does not arise from work, be abolished.* **[Rich people don't deserve their money]**

12. *Since every war imposes on the people fearful sacrifices in blood and treasure, all personal profit arising from the war must be regarded as treason to the people. We therefore demand the total confiscation of all war profits.*

13. *We demand the nationalization of all trusts.* **[Government control of wealth]**

192

14. We demand profit-sharing in large industries. **[Corporations can't make money]**

15. We demand a generous increase in old-age pensions. **[Free guaranteed retirement]**

16. We demand the creation and maintenance of a sound middle-class, the immediate communalization of large stores which will be rented cheaply to small tradespeople, and the strongest consideration must be given to ensure that small traders shall deliver the supplies needed by the State, the provinces and municipalities. **[Government takeover of large businesses]**

17. We demand an agrarian reform in accordance with our national requirements, and the enactment of a law to expropriate the owners without compensation of any land needed for the common purpose. The abolition of ground rents, and the

prohibition of all speculation in land.
[Government control and seizure of land]

18. *We demand that ruthless war be waged against those who work to the injury of the common welfare. Traitors, usurers, profiteers, etc., are to be punished with death, regardless of creed or race.*

19. *We demand that Roman law, which serves a materialist ordering of the world, be replaced by German common law.*

20. *In order to make it possible for every capable and industrious German to obtain higher education, and thus the opportunity to reach into positions of leadership, the State must assume the responsibility of organizing thoroughly the entire cultural system of the people. The curricula of all educational establishments shall be adapted to practical life. The conception of the State Idea (science of citizenship) must be taught in the schools from the very beginning. We demand that specially*

194

talented children of poor parents, whatever their station or occupation, be educated at the expense of the State. **[Free education]**

21. The State has the duty to help raise the standard of national health by providing maternity welfare centers, by prohibiting juvenile labor, by increasing physical fitness through the introduction of compulsory games and gymnastics, and by the greatest possible encouragement of associations concerned with the physical education of the young. **[Free Healthcare especially for women and the young]**

22. We demand the abolition of the regular army and the creation of a national (folk) army.

23. We demand that there be a legal campaign against those who propagate deliberate political lies and disseminate them through the press. In order to make possible the creation of a German press, we demand: **[Censoring of media and dissemination of information]**

(a) All editors and their assistants on newspapers published in the German language shall be German citizens.

(b) Non-German newspapers shall only be published with the express permission of the State. They must not be published in the German language.

(c) All financial interests in or in any way affecting German newspapers shall be forbidden to non-Germans by law, and we demand that the punishment for transgressing this law be the immediate suppression of the newspaper and the expulsion of the non-Germans from the Reich.

Newspapers transgressing against the common welfare shall be suppressed. We demand legal action against those tendencies in art and literature that have a disruptive influence upon the life of our folk, and that any organizations that offend against the foregoing demands shall be dissolved. **[censoring any language deemed offensive in art and literature –** Banning conservatives from Social Media, and from T.V. shows like "Last Man Standing" are literally Nazi tactics]

196

24. *We demand freedom for all religious faiths in the state, insofar as they do not endanger its existence or offend the moral and ethical sense of the Germanic race.*

The party as such represents the point of view of a positive Christianity [complete falsehood as no Christian documents or books agree with the Nazi view of race or government] *without binding itself to any one particular confession.* [A nice way of saying, "you can't hold us to any particular belief or ideal"] *It fights against the Jewish materialist spirit within and without, and is convinced that a lasting recovery of our folk can only come about from within on the principle:*

COMMON GOOD BEFORE INDIVIDUAL GOOD **[It takes a village, not parents]**

25. *In order to carry out this program we demand: the creation of a strong central authority in the State, the unconditional authority by the political central parliament of the whole State and all its organizations.* **[Jack booted thugs]**

The formation of professional committees and of committees representing the several estates of the realm, to ensure that the laws promulgated by the central authority shall be carried out by the federal states.

The leaders of the party undertake to promote the execution of the foregoing points at all costs, if necessary at the sacrifice of their own lives.[49] [Encouraging a religious zeal]

Does this sound like a particular ideology that you would like? Free housing, free healthcare, free education, a living wage for all, and free retirement are all part of the pre-requisite for government control of individuals and ultimately tyranny. Did you notice that the Nazi platform required a censoring of any language that they deemed offensive? Isn't that political correctness, and doesn't that go against our 1st Amendment right to free speech?

Pay special attention to the "Common good before individual good" line. It shows that if it is determined that something is for the common good, then your individual rights, property, and freedom don't matter. The Nazis knew that in order for this to work, they needed a "Strong central authority" and to enforce their beliefs "at all costs".

This led to the formation of "committees" of brown shirts and enforcers who carried out their plan, censored the media, and violently took what they felt to be in the best interest of the state. They engaged in book burnings and disrupted rallies and meetings where people disagreed with them. Does this remind you of Antifa? It should. They do exactly what the Nazis did, and in the name of being against Nazis.

Think about the book burnings and censoring of the media of that day. It is exactly what happens in our national news media. Anyone who disagrees with the progressive opinion is shouted down and derided. Speakers are attacked to attempt to silence them. Colleges and companies are boycotted if they dare have a speaker that voices ideas against the accepted standard. People lose jobs over voicing a political opinion in America today. A black conservative by the name of Candace Owens was attacked and shouted out of a restaurant because she dared to speak out against the idea of White Privilege. She was called a white supremacist.[54] These are fascist acts. That is the Nazi tactic.

Social media like Facebook and Twitter both have admitted to seeking out dissenting opinions and banning those people, or shutting down their accounts. This type of censoring is fascist as well. At the time this book was written, I have had several of my accounts banned for stating facts like what you find in this book. On election night 2016, as I was replying to a post, Facebook permanently banned my account due to simple facts posted about the corruption of Hillary Clinton. This is fascism.

How Not to be a Nazi

If you ever find yourself shouting down someone or hurling insults in a debate or discussion, stop. Take a deep breath. Think about a logical argument and then make that argument in a respectful manner.

If you ever find yourself advocating for something free, stop. Realize that somebody will be paying for it. Realize that in all likelihood, the money will be taken without their consent. Realize that you are not actually advocating for free things, but for theft. The government does not produce anything, it TAKES. Everything given away by the government is stolen from the citizens by threat of force. If you don't pay your taxes, the IRS will send the police to your house to either take you or your possessions.

The police have guns. If you resist, you most likely will be shot. The free healthcare that you demand is actually taken by force from others. Remember that America was started in part due to the British enforcing their unfair taxes by sending soldiers to collect. Never advocate for the government giving something for free, it's not free.

Free healthcare requires doctors and nurses to work for you without you personally paying for it. This is essentially slave labor. When the government steps in and demands doctors and nurses give you healthcare, they are requiring people to perform a service at whatever compensation the government deems fair, not what the doctors deem fair. This is state controlled industry. This is socialism. The government can then randomly change prices or lower prices until the practitioners can no longer afford to give that service and then the government completely takes it over to keep providing it. The government NEVER does something as well, as cost effective, or as efficiently as a privately run business does.

Socialism has never worked in any country it has been tried in. People will point to Sweden and Norway as examples but those are not good examples. Both countries offer free healthcare and free college, but they are still capitalist countries where the government does not have control of industry. However, if that is all you want, know that they both have income tax rates over 50% and sales tax rates of almost 25%. You may make $28 an hour but you only get to spend $7 of it. Do you still want that kind of Democratic Socialism?

In Conclusion, if you don't want to be like Hitler and Nazi Germany there are basically three things you must not do.

1. Don't be a socialist.
2. Don't be a fascist that prevents others from voicing dissenting points of view.
3. Don't advocate for the government (the many) over the individual.

Freedom is predicated upon the rights of personal property, free speech, the rights of the individual, and the capability to defend them all.

Chapter 8: Hope for America

"We hold these truths to be self-evident, that all men are created equal, that they are endowed by their Creator with certain unalienable Rights, that among these are Life, Liberty and the pursuit of Happiness.--That to secure these rights, Governments are instituted among Men, deriving their just powers from the consent of the governed, --That whenever any Form of Government becomes destructive of these ends, it is the Right of the People to alter or to abolish it, and to institute new Government..." – The Declaration of Independence July 4th,1776

The first slaves were brought to the Americas in 1617 in Virginia. This is an undisputed historical fact. America didn't start until 1776. America is not responsible for slavery. America rose out of the ashes of a rebellion against the most powerful nation on Earth at the time, England. They knew slavery was wrong, and yet it had been a way of life on this continent under the King for over 150 years.

A true study of history shows, that though several founding fathers had inherited and possessed slaves of their own, they abhorred the trade and did all they could to treat theirs fairly. Caring for them, seeing to their well-being, and often writing home about them when they were away ensuring the establishment of the new country was common. In a world where slavery was the accepted practice, America's founding fathers were radicals who dared to argue against it even before they started a Revolution. [50]

An Old Hope

Here are some of our founding fathers words which may shed some light on the reason that they put the words "ALL MEN ARE CREATED EQUAL" into their Declaration of Independence from the crown.[51]

"The augmentation of slaves weakens the states; and such a trade is diabolical in itself, and disgraceful to mankind."

-- **George Mason**

*"Bigotry is the disease of ignorance, or
morbid minds; enthusiasm of the free and
buoyant. Education and free discussion are
the antidotes of both."*

-- **Thomas Jefferson**, *Thomas Jefferson
Papers, Library of Congress, Manuscript
Division, 1816*

*"I believe a time will come when an
opportunity will be offered to abolish this
lamentable evil."*

-- **Patrick Henry**, *letter to Robert Pleasants,
January 18, 1773*

*"Nothing is more certainly written in the book
of fate than that these people are to be free."*

-- **Thomas Jefferson**, *Autobiography, 1821*

*"There is not a man living who wishes more
sincerely than I do, to see a plan adopted for
the abolition of it."*

-- **George Washington**, *letter to Robert Morris, April 12, 1786*

"Every measure of prudence, therefore, ought to be assumed for the eventual total extirpation of slavery from the United States ... I have, throughout my whole life, held the practice of slavery in ... abhorrence."

-- **John Adams**, *letter to Robert Evans, June 8, 1819*

"It is much to be wished that slavery may be abolished. The honour of the States, as well as justice and humanity, in my opinion, loudly call upon them to emancipate these unhappy people. To contend for our own liberty, and to deny that blessing to others, involves an inconsistency not to be excused."

--**John Jay**, *letter to R. Lushington, March 15, 1786*

"Another of my wishes is to depend as little as possible on the labour of slaves."

-- **James Madison**, *Letter to R. H. Lee, July 17, 1785 (Madison, 1865, I, page 161)*

"[I]f slavery, as a national evil, is to be abolished [No matter the cost], *and it be just that it be done at the national expense, the amount of the expense is not a paramount consideration."*

-- **James Madison**, *Letter to Robert J. Evans*

As proof that this great new nation intended to be a free haven for all, America begin to dismantle the horrible slave trade shortly after we achieved our freedom.

"It were doubtless to be wished, that the power of prohibiting the importation of slaves had not been postponed until the year 1808, or rather that it had been suffered to have immediate operation. But it is not difficult to account, either for this restriction on the general government, or for the manner in which the whole clause is expressed. It ought to be considered as a great point gained in favor of humanity, that a period of twenty years may terminate

forever, within these States, a traffic which has so long and so loudly upbraided the barbarism of modern policy; that within that period, it will receive a considerable discouragement from the federal government, and may be totally abolished, by a concurrence of the few States which continue the unnatural traffic, in the prohibitory example which has been given by so great a majority of the Union. Happy would it be for the unfortunate Africans, if an equal prospect lay before them of being redeemed from the oppressions of their European brethren!"

-- **James Madison**,
Federalist Paper No. 42

Slavery and racism was never intended by our forefathers. At the very founding of our nation they wrote into our founding documents a reverence for life and freedom. Abraham Lincoln rightly pointed this out in his many debates against slavery.

"I think the authors of that notable instrument intended to include all men, but they did not intend to declare all men equal

in all respects. They did not mean to say all were equal in color, size, intellect, moral development, or social capacity. They defined with tolerable distinctness, in what respects they did consider all men created equal—equal in 'certain inalienable rights, among which were life, liberty, and the pursuit of happiness.'... They meant to set up a standard maxim for free society, which should be familiar to all, and revered by all; constantly looked to, constantly labored for, and even though never perfectly attained, constantly approximated, and thereby constantly spreading and deepening its influence." - June 26, 1857, in Springfield, Illinois, referring to the Declaration of Independence

"An inspection of the Constitution will show that the right of property in a slave is not 'distinctly and expressly affirmed' in it." - February 27, 1860 Speech at the Cooper Institute

"That is the real issue. That is the issue that will continue in this country when these poor tongues of Judge Douglas and

*myself shall be silent. It is the eternal struggle between these two principles -- right and wrong -- throughout the world. They are the two principles that have stood face to face from the beginning of time, and will ever continue to struggle. The one is the common right of humanity and the other the divine right of kings. It is the same principle in whatever shape it develops itself. It is the same spirit that says, '**You work and toil and earn bread, and I'll eat it**'. No matter in what shape it comes, whether from the mouth of a king who seeks to bestride the people of his own nation and live by the fruit of their labor, or from one race of men as an apology for enslaving another race, **it is the same tyrannical principle**.*" - October 15, 1858 Debate at Alton, Illinois

"Four score and seven years ago our fathers brought forth on this continent, a new nation, conceived in Liberty, and dedicated to the proposition that all men are created equal". - November 19, 1863 Gettysburg Address

"Every advocate of slavery naturally desires to see blasted, and crushed, the liberty promised the black man by the new constitution." -November 14, 1864 Letter to Stephen A. Hurlbut

"One eighth of the whole population were colored slaves, not distributed generally over the Union, but localized in the Southern part of it. These slaves constituted a peculiar and powerful interest. All knew that this interest was, somehow, the cause of the war."
- March 4, 1865 Inaugural Address

America is the only nation to have fought a Civil War to end the practice of slavery. We were not founded on the backs of slaves. America rose like a Phoenix out of the ashes of tyranny and quickly moved to abolish that horrible practice at ALL costs, to the tune of 620,000 American lives, most of whom were white.

Nowhere else in human history will you see a race or a nation of people so willing to see freedom of another group of people that they spilled that much of their own blood to make it happen.

Shortly after that, we enshrined in our Constitution the 13th, 14, and 15th Amendment to ensure slavery and racism never came back to America, the land that has always loved freedom and liberty. As explained in this book, a segment of our population, which I am loathe to call fellow Americans, did all they could to relegate the black population to second-class people. In 1964, America passed the Civil Rights Act to force Democrats to treat people as equals in public life. They only had to do that because 100 years earlier the Democrats blocked it and enacted Jim Crow laws.

Since that date, racism has not been allowed legally in America and every instance of public and institutional racism has been outlawed. In most of our lifetimes (in 2018), racism has NOT been institutionalized or accepted.

Individual racism will always be around because immorality cannot be legislated against, nor can the thoughts or heart of mankind be regulated without tyranny. However, America has done all that a free nation can do to stop racism against minorities.

A New Hope

America has a unique history rooted in freedom of the individual and equal treatment under the law. Lady Justice is a common underlying theme in our laws and at our courthouses. She is most commonly portrayed as a blindfolded woman carrying a sword and a set of scales. This statue represents the fair and equal administration of law, without corruption, greed, prejudice, or favor. This means that all laws apply equally to all men and women regardless of race, religion, creed, status, or money.

America is resilient and her people are independent and free thinkers. We abhor tyranny and being told what to do or think, especially by those who consider themselves better than us. I have hope that we will learn from the past, despite what our Media, Government, and Schools try to make us do. I have hope that people will wake up to the indoctrination and not allow it to change our nation for the worse.

America is and always has been a melting pot that affords each citizen the opportunity to become a productive person and make themselves successful in whatever way they choose. This does not and should not diminish a person's reverence for their heritage. We should always teach history and respect each other's origins and family heritage, but the nation as a whole needs to have its own unique heritage in order to survive. Either you are American or you are not.

No more should we label ourselves as American this, or American that. You can be a black person in America and have great respect for and great pride in your African heritage, but to call yourself African-American does a disservice to both countries. You should be proud of and willing to identify with the country that you choose to be a citizen of. The same holds true for any other kind of hyphenated American.

There is not room for a divided loyalty or for separating Americans into subgroups like that in a great nation that unites all its citizens under the banner of Freedom for all!

"When you open your heart to patriotism, there is no room for prejudice."

"It is time to remember that old wisdom our soldiers will never forget: that whether

we are black or brown or white, we all bleed the same red blood of patriots, we all enjoy the same glorious freedoms, and we all salute the same great American Flag."

- Inaugural Address January 20, 2016 by President Trump

"No dream is too big. No challenge is too great. Nothing we want for our future is beyond our reach." [52] *- President Trump*

We are one people, with one common heritage of Liberty and Justice for All. Let's act like it. Be an American. Be proud of that heritage of excellence, fighting for freedom, and always standing against those who would enslave your mind or your body.

God Bless America

and

May God Bless You

- C. K. Justice

Documentation

1 Family Violence Statistics pg. 13
   https://www.bjs.gov/content/pub/pdf/fvs02.pdf

2. Reason in Common Sense CH12 by George Santayan

3. www.cherokee.org/About-The-Nation/History/Trail-of-Tears/A-Brief-History-of-the-Trail-of-Tears

4. Encyclopedia Britannica Vol.12 pg.763, 16th edition 1991

5. http://www.history.com/news/when-america-despised-the-irish-the-19th-centurys-refugee-crisis

6. Library of Congress
   https://www.loc.gov/teachers/classroommaterials/presentationsandactivities/presentations/immigration/irish5.html#

7. U.S.A. Census Bureau
   https://www.census.gov/newsroom/releases/archives/facts_for_features_special_editions/cb11-ff03.html

8. Office of the Historian,
   https://history.state.gov/milestones/1866-
   1898/chinese-immigration

9. http://www.asiannation.org/korean.shtm
   l#sthash.a0muGAlT.DLJocPzN.dpbs

10. http://www.history.com/topics/us-immigration-
    since-1965

11. Public Broadcasting Service,
    http://www.pbs.org/thewar/at_home_civil_rights_j
    apanese_american.htm

12. The University of California -
    https://calisphere.org/exhibitions/essay/8/relocatio
    n/ and https://www.congress.gov/bill/100th-
    congress/house-bill/442

13. History.com - http://www.history.com/this-day-
    in-history/texas-declares-independence

14. http://aliengearholsters.com/blog/molon-labe-
    meaning/

15. http://www.theclever.com/15-countries-where-
    slavery-is-still-legal/ and
    https://borgenproject.org/countries-that-still-have-
    slavery/ and
    http://www.worldatlas.com/articles/countries-with-
    the-most-modern-slaves-today.html

16. History.com
http://www.history.com/topics/black-history/underground-railroad

17. The American Presidency Project
http://www.presidency.ucsb.edu/ws/index.php?pid=29620

18. Encyclopedia Britannica
https://www.britannica.com/event/Jim-Crow-law

19. Washington Post
https://www.washingtonpost.com/archive/politics/2005/06/19/a-senators-shame

20. Anatomy of the SS State, published by Paladin, 1970, pp.29-30 by Helmut Krausnick and Martin Broszat

21. Cable News Network
http://www.cnn.com/2017/10/25/politics/bowe-bergdahl-sentencing-hearing/index.html

22. Encyclopedia Britannica https://www.britannica.com/topic/Republican-Party

23. Constitutional Rights Foundation http://www.crf-usa.org/black-history-month/slavery-in-the-american-south

24. Mein Kampf, Adolf Hitler – English edition Copyright 2014 by White Wolf (Translated by James Murphy, Abbots Langley, February 1939)

25. Archives.gov
https://www.archives.gov/legislative/features/civil-rights-1964/senate-roll-call.html

26. Dinesh D'Souza
dineshdsouza.com/news/big-switch-big-lie/

27. ChristainPost.com
https://www.christianpost.com/news/hitler-was-not-a-christian-164397/

28. Townhall.com
https://townhall.com/columnists/walterewilliams/2018/08/08/colleges-a-force-for-evil-n2507178

29. Washington Examiner
https://www.washingtonexaminer.com/walter-williams-college-professors-can-teach-you-to-hate-america

30. Thought Catalog
https://thoughtcatalog.com/emily-goldstein/2015/05/get-rid-of-white-people/

31. Truth and Action
http://www.truthandaction.org/mass-college-professor-white-males-are-a-cancer-and-must-die-urges-students-to-kill-themselves/

32. Chicago Tribune
https://www.chicagotribune.com/news/columnists/
glanton/ct-met-white-privilege-dahleen-glanton-
20180328-story.html

33. Huffington Post
https://www.huffingtonpost.com/entry/opinion-
white-women-gop-midterms-white-
supremacy_us_5bef0f98e4b0b84243e23e3b

34. ABC News
abcnews.go.com/2020/story?id=2629192&page=1

35. NBC News
https://www.nbcnews.com/think/opinion/white-
people-are-still-raised-be-racially-illiterate-if-we-
ncna906646

36. NBC News
https://www.nbcnews.com/news/nbcblk/oped-
white-people-it-s-time-use-your-privilege-whether-
n804361

37. Brainy Quote
brainyquote.com/authors/Maxine_waters

38. AZ Quotes -
https://www.azquotes.com/author/6819-
Eric_Holder

39. Washington Times

https://www.washingtontimes.com/news/2011/mar/3/eric-holders-liberal-racism/

40. Brainy Quote -
https://www.brainyquote.com/authors/cory_booker

41. The Guardian July 31/2001

42. "The 20 Worst Quotes from Louis Farrakhan –
Liberal Americas Favorite Racist" The Townhall –
March/24/2018

43. LA Times August 16, 2017 "President Obama
often spoke about race relations in the U.S. Here
are some of his words"

44. Quotetab.com

45. Noqreport.com October 20, 2017

46. Washington Examiner June 13, 2017

47. CBSnews.com July 6, 2018
"Man sentenced for hate crime in live-streamed
beating of mentally disabled teen"

48. Personal interview with WWII Soldier Gerard
Stephany 1999, documented in research paper
titled "The Atomic Bomb" at IPFW

49. History Place

http://www.historyplace.com/worldwar2/riseofhitler/25points.htm

50. https://www.revolutionary-war.net/slavery-and-the-founding-fathers.html

51. George Mason University
econfaculty.gmu.edu/wew/quotes/slavery.html

52. Brainy Quotes
www.brainyquote.com/authors/donald_trump

53. Personal interview with Emily Stephany

54. Independent.co.uk – 7 August 2018
"Candace Owens: Prominent Trump supporters chased out of restaurant by protesters"

55. New York Times
https://www.nytimes.com/2016/12/14/nyregion/manhattan-yasmin-seweid-false-hate-crime.html

56. ABC News – 24 May 2018
https://www.abc.net.au/news/2018-05-24/kendrick-lamar-n-word-hip-hop-inevitable/9794446

THANK YOU

As a reader, you now have the ability to influence others by taking a few moments to rate this book. Login to Amazon and take a few moments to tell the author and others your thoughts about:
"American Racism
Black Power in a White World"

For more real talk about current events and other issues affecting America, please check out my blog and join my email list at:

www.Angrypatriot42.com

You can also follow me on twitter
@CKJustice_AP42

Or on Facebook
Facebook.com/CKJusticeAP42

Look for my other titles on Amazon:

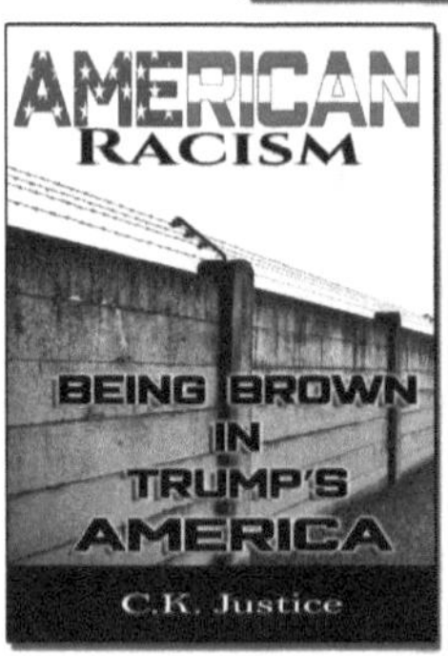

226

Biography

Born in the Midwest and raised by a blue collar worker, CK learned the value of hard work and "raising yourself up by your own boot straps". His high school years were spent in the ghetto of a large city going to an inner-city school where he experienced racism on almost a daily basis.

Realizing after graduating, there were only two options for him, he chose a third option. He joined the Army as an infantryman. Experiencing the plights of other nations brought knowledge and a greater respect for freedom to C.K.

After getting out of the military, he began working in the financial sector where racism forced him out of his job. Taking his career on another course, that of education, has led to the present day. When not writing, C.K. enjoys reading and spending time with his family in the West.